US Copyright - Anonymous Child ©
Registration Number: **TXu 1-830-156**

Certificate of Registration

This Certificate issued under the seal of the Copyright Office in accordance with title 17, *United States Code*, attests that registration has been made for the work identified below. The information on this certificate has been made a part of the Copyright Office records.

Maria A. Pallante

Register of Copyrights, United States of America

Registration Number

TXu 1-830-156

Effective date of registration:

August 29, 2012

Title

Title of Work: Anonymous Child

Completion/Publication

Year of Completion: 2012

International Standard Number: ISBN

Author

Author: Bruce David Hubbell

Author Created: text, compilation, editing

Work made for hire: No

Citizen of: United States   **Domiciled in:** United States

Year Born: 1944

Copyright claimant

Copyright Claimant: Bruce David Hubbell

469 Winding Wood Way, Sebastopol, CA, 95472, United States

Rights and Permissions

Organization Name: david productions, LLC

Name: Bruce David Hubbell

Email: hubbell@comcast.net   **Telephone:** 707-823-3076

Address: 469 Winding Wood Way

Sebastopol, CA 95472 United States

Certification

Name: Bruce David Hubbell

Date: August 29, 2012

<u>THE THIRD STEP PRAYER</u>

God, I offer myself to Thee - To build with me and to do with me as Thou wilt. Relieve me of the bondage of self, that I may better do Thy will. Take away my difficulties that victory over them may bear witness to those I would help of Thy Power, Thy Love, and Thy Way of life. May I do Thy will always!

ANONYMOUS CHILD

david productions LLC
469 Winding Wood Way
Sebastopol, Ca 95472
USA
www.anonymouschild.org

© Bruce David Hubbell

ISBN-13: 978-0989571906
ISBN-10: 0989571904

Editing & Copy; design supervision: Kristen House - http://kristencorrects.com

Art & Cover; design supervision: Richard Stodart - http://richardstodart.com

Website development & design supervision: Sigurfreyr Jónasson - http://www.nordicwolf.com/

So our troubles, we think, are basically of our own making. They arise out of ourselves, and the alcoholic is an extreme example of self-will run riot, though he usually doesn't think so. Above everything, we alcoholics must be rid of this selfishness. We must, or it kills us! God makes that possible. And there often seems no way of entirely getting rid of self without His aid. Many of us had moral and philosophical convictions galore, but we could not live up to them even though we would have liked to. Neither could we reduce our self-centeredness much by wishing or trying on our own power. We had to have God's help.

This is the how and why of it. First of all, we had to quit playing God. It didn't work. Next, we decided that hereafter in this drama of life, God was going to be our Director. He is the Principal; we are His agents. He is the Father, and we are His children. Most good ideas are simple, and this concept was the keystone of the new and triumphant arch through which we passed to freedom.

When we sincerely took such a position, all sorts of remarkable things followed. We had a new Employer. Being all powerful, He provided what we needed, if we kept close to Him and performed His work well. Established on such a footing we became less and less interested in ourselves, our little plans and designs. More and more we became interested in seeing what we could contribute to life. As we felt new power flow in, as we enjoyed peace of mind, as we discovered we could face life successfully, as we became conscious of His presence, we began to lose our fear of today, tomorrow or the hereafter. We were reborn.

We were now at Step Three. Many of us said to our Maker, as we understood Him: **"God, I offer myself to Thee-to build with me and to do with me as Thou wilt. Relieve me of the bondage of self, that I may better do Thy will. Take away my difficulties, that victory over them may bear witness to those I would help of Thy Power, Thy Love, and Thy Way of life. May I do Thy will always!"** *We thought well before taking this step making sure we were ready; that we could at last abandon ourselves utterly to Him.*

We found it very desirable to take this spiritual step with an understanding person, such as our wife, best friend or spiritual adviser. But it is better to meet God alone than with one who might misunderstand. The wording was, of course, quite optional so long as we expressed the idea, voicing it without reservation. This was only a beginning, though if honestly and humbly made, an effect, sometimes a very great one, was felt at once.

Next we launched out on a course of vigorous action, the first step of which is a personal housecleaning: ***A Moral Inventory*** *. . . . THE FOURTH STEP . .::*

Friday, December 21, 2007 (personal memoir)
Now It Begins

Over the last 35 years I have been attracted to the inherent authentic wisdom and practices of current and ancient religions and spiritual traditions. I am utterly fascinated by the stories and lives of saints and realizers detailing their sufferings and awakenings. I am continually compelled by the mysteries, intrigue and adventures I experience personally discovering, firsthand, the truth and principles of human life and God.

I am a spiritual seeker.

On September 27, 1944 I was born and baptized into a large intimate and loving Irish Catholic clan in Detroit, Michigan. I was the sole child between Stuart and Evelyn Hubbell; I was the mutual brother to my father's three children — Dick, Jim, and Francie — and my mother's daughter, Ruthie. My parents met in 1938 and were married in 1940.

They were both recovering alcoholics — their adulthood spent in AA. And even so, I grew up and became an alcoholic myself.

I was gifted with spiritually sensitive relatives. My grandmother was a genuine matriarch of the clan. She brought all 4'11" of her powerful personality to deeply and religiously effect with her behavior three generations — all 72 of us — with love, her use of the word of God and with impeccable Catholic formal practices and holy day observations. Most of the time she carried her rosary around her wrist, almost always when sitting. When many of us grandchildren and even my father her first child would come and see her on her back porch…It would be the custom — we would greet her with laying our heads in her lap — she would sometimes rub our backs or talk "with us" in those chest close meetings and when she would be silent and, "Humm," and this would be the sign to be quiet and just be still and feel her and all the moment and she would extemporaneously pray to Jesus and God — she always insisted on holding us close or kissing us on the mouth and telling us she loved us as we looked into her clear happy, joyous and playful blue eyes — these loving eyes I had looked into and these gentle wise powerful arms I had felt since my birth. As a child and into my teens my parents or my father would take me to church every Sunday. I would sit next to him and follow the rituals. Then we would…"after church go to Grandma's house on the way home for a visit." We rarely missed going over to grandma's or meet her at one of my relatives every Sunday — And every Sunday was the always accountable, unspoken agreed upon, Sunday church attendance requirement as a Catholic. This time with my dad and mom and family was always a pleasure, interesting, and sometimes delightfully brief. It was accepted if the men greeted each other with a mouth kiss; nothing to think about.

I was blessed with my very caring, kind, gentle, loving and my first best friend, my Spiritually conscientious sister, who at 17 ran away from home in her own pursuit of union with Jesus' calling to him and to become a Dominican nun — and she still is to this day.

My cousin, too, was extraordinary in his stated feelings for God and Christ. He also demonstrated to all of us at an early age such a living spiritual conversion and attraction to commune and serve God that we knew before he knew he was going to be a priest — he went off to seminary at 14 and in his last year, fell in love, and chose to leave a year before ordination to become married.

I observed and practiced Catholicism with all of the rituals of confirmation, confession, contrition and communion as a child. My religious childhood and young adult influences were from my family that was a practicing and solid Catholic clan of God: We were grounded, as a family, in a Spiritually based lifestyle, demonstrating mutual love and acceptance — an undisturbed time of pure family bonding in a true family of Roman Catholics who genuinely practiced full rituals of ceremonial devotion to God, Jesus and Holy Spirit with each other.

But now — in looking back with clearer eye and understanding I see maybe it was the combination of the hypocrisies that caused confusion in my feelings. There was my family and our feeling practices and agreements in our approach to God; opposed to what I witnessed in the loose adult educators and longtime resident students while attending Catholic schools or experiencing the new global awareness and intense cultural transformations of the 60's as an adolescent teen that I slowly (and now I see I would never say it) became a doubting youthful agnostic.

In the 70s I was made emotionally vulnerable by deep feelings of social chaos; and after seven years of marriage, at 25, the uncontested divorce creating the loss of my high school sweetheart, our trust and genuine intimate contact including my daughters of four and six.

I, too, at that time, I was deeply impacted by others my age speaking words, sharing their deeper feelings and meanings through their radical music combined with finding esoteric books with writings and clues to this current evolving Aquarian Age coming out of New Thought.

I craved more information and experiences of Spiritual disciplines through the Eastern approaches of communing with God; and I first heard the concepts of consciousness and enlightenment. I began to desire to manage my own free will by directing my attention & sitting quietly in meditation using the mantric techniques of Transcendental Meditation and the teachings of Maharishi Mahesh Yogi.

I began understanding and practicing the healing principles of conscious eating, exercise and experiencing the deep healing power and transforming effects of direct non-sexual massage touch. I participated in EST and many growth groups for 10 years; personally serving Werner Erhard. My head was blessed by the 16th Gyalwa Karmapa, Rangjung Rigpe Dorje in the Black Crown Ceremony where a monk tied a neck tight red braid mala I wore unremoved for over a year.

I became a student practitioner and actively participated in the community of Adidam for 20 years receiving many teaching gifts of seva-selfless service, darshan kundalini meditation in satsang with profound feelings of deep neurological and psychic purifications by the bhakti-yoga when personally serving Adi Da, my Beloved, my Guru in the Sangha of his devotees, many now my dearest friends. I had a one-on-one lunch with Ram Dass only to discover he still had moments of unconsciousness with his own addictions, similar to my own.

In 1987, I became a practicing alcoholic for 14 years to cope with psychic, emotional and the continuing spiritual growth pains of my own unconsciousness. But is truly only by divine grace I began to be attracted to recover my moral and emotional sanity through the practices, intimate fellowship and rigors of the social accountability of consistent daily practices, having a sponsor and working the 12 Steps, including the honor of helping other alcoholic sponsees in Alcoholics Anonymous.

This is the story I wish to tell of a recovered alcoholic…

…a VERY grateful recover**ED** alcoholic!

Authors Note: April 10, 2013

If you have access to the audio version of Anonymous Child...I highly recommend that you **LISTEN** to that first...

I am the author and I feel blessed to have the privilege to be the orator of this event. I want this to be a bit of the formality to which I launch into this story. But before that can happen, you must understand the background of my childhood and how it launched me into my life.

Please note what you are about to read is a written, unedited for meaning, transcription of 10 hours (recorded on a hand held recorder, usually in my car traveling) of **AA TALKS**...more to me; **DISCOVERY** talks...spontaneous and extemporaneous talks...allowing my speaking about my life; having recovered from alcoholism...and here...making amends for my alcoholic behavior.

...I have not allowed any changing of words for meanings...there have been some slight paragraph formatting to allow the transcriber to format according to their skills and perceptions.

The original audio presentation is identical to what you are about to read...**BUT SO MUCH IS MISSING**...Part of the **MOST IMPORTANT** intended impact for the **LISTENER; THAT PART** is missing ...because of the emotional nature of my personal spontaneous revelations I experienced...as I told the story. THAT PART...is missing here reading.

I am speaking directly to the alcoholic addict and the unconscious addict in us all...to open up **LISTENING**...to allow **LISTENING** to guide us! ...**TO LEARN TO TRUST** ourselves again...maybe for the first time!

This is not a novel or a story but what you are about to read is a journey — a journey I traveled, in real time.

I began these 85 AA talks on Saturday January 7, 2012 at 11:15 am and I stopped on January 15, 2012 at 4am.

Anonymous Child

A Spontaneous Oral Memoir

. . . listening to the speaking of sanity

"Speaking to the Heart of the Matter of Sobriety"

A recovered alcoholics tale of the timeless lessons for anyone to discover
the Always Present Superior Force of Life; the demonstration of IT's
. . . Laws for Love: which Allow Us to BE & Feel & Know . . .
WE ARE Already Whole and Already Complete
without any words or meanings

Jimmy Murtaugh – took this photo . . .my friend

My 4th & my mother's 37th Birthday Party - all AA members
September 27, 1948

Tommy Isles; my dad's sponsee, Mae Morgan; my mom's sponsee :
My dad with his hands on his hips, smiling away
Bill Burke; my dad sponsor "my Best Pal" . . . I've got my hand on
Mary Burke; my mother's sponsor
. . .and my devoted loving mother. . .

Dedicated to Stuart & Evelyn Hubbell

To pass on the recovery processes of learning:
What is SERENITY?
What is ACCEPTANCE?
What is COURAGE?
What is WISDOM?
then…
What is it…to KNOW THE DIFFERENCE?

THAT DIFFERENCE TO KNOW CHANGE: serenity, acceptance, courage and wisdom…I witnessed the practicing of those principles demonstrated in the living with and loving with Stuart & Evelyn Hubbell…in their over 50 years of AA recovery work—my mom and my dad.

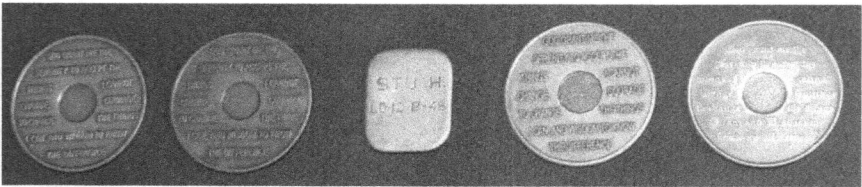

My Father's First Year AA Medallion: STU H. LD 12-8-46

My 24 Hour, One Year, Four Year, and My Mother's 50 Year Chip

My Fathers Passion : Hunting for fish and game OUTDOORS

My Mothers Passion: Hunting for hearts & souls INDOORS

Angeles. My remembrance is that at the end of that meeting, he told me he had to shake hands with at least 3,500 people.

"Bob always would tell us the number of months and the number of years and the number of days since he had his last drink. He visited us at our house once with his wife and once after he'd lost his wife, and we visited him at Akron.

"One of the outstanding incidents of my life is the Sunday we spent with him at his home in Akron. It was something like people coming to Lourdes—people he'd never seen or heard of. One was a dean of a large college in Ohio. Two people who stand out in my memory were a lawyer and his wife. They had driven all the way from Detroit to tell him what he had done through A.A. for them. This woman, who was charming, had been on skid row, and we couldn't believe it. She wanted to tell Bob, with tears in her eyes, how she went down to a reformatory in Detroit every Sunday and preached [sic], and she was very proud the last three Sundays. She'd had practically the whole attendance of the reformatory, while the minister who had come out to preach a sermon had only two or three people.

"I don't know how many people came that day in Akron. There were seven or eight—entirely unknown to him before—who just came to his house to express their gratitude, and that was the way it was everywhere he went.

INTRODUCTION, PROLOGUES & MY PARENTS

Alcoholism is a Disease

Finding Responsible Freedom, with Honor, in the Messages of Alcoholism

My Mom — a Sponsor

My Dad — a Sponsor

THE CHILDREN – That's What This is All About

PROLOGUE — An Offering of My Selfish Gift

NOW IT BEGINS — The Gift of your Listening to Me for ME

OUR CONTRITION — BE A Confessional; BE the Heart of Listening

WHERE TO START

Talks – Sequential in Time

1 — I Want to be an Alcoholic When I Grow Up...

2 — My First Sights of Living Alcoholics & Their Consistent Behavior

3 — Frank D — Our Live-in Alcoholic Carpenter

4 — Tommy I — Demonstrates the Edge of the Question of Recovery

5 — The LIVES of the Liquid Alcohol, Beer, and Wine

6 — 1962 — My First Time Getting Drunk, & the Warning Unnoticed

7 — 1962 — My Honor Uncovered...A Silent Integrity Fights Back

8 — 1963 — Life's Commitments Takeover

9 — 1964 — Opportunity Calls — MSU — The Cost of Hidden FUN — 40 Years' Worth

10 — 2001 — 37 Years to Take My First Step — In five minutes I Committed to be a Sponsor

11 — 2001 — I Turn it OVER

12 — 1964 — The Journey to my Freedom & Sanity Begins on the Road Less Traveled

13 – PERSONAL Side Note – For Honesty and Thoroughness

14 – 1965 – The Space of No Space

15 – 1965 – Deeper Found Intimacy

16 – 1965 – White Castle and Her

17 – 1965 – In the Dark – Turning Away from My Father

18 – REVEALING the CORE LISTENING of RECOVERY

19 – REMEMBER – Shine to the CHILDREN and Those Who Wish to Recover

20 – Freedom of Tribal Order & Real Joy of Conscious Growth

21 – Imprinting the True Natural Ecstatic Speech from My Maternal Lineage

22 – Contain Celebration Display to the Children

23 – In the HEART of the MATTER of LOVE

24 – 1965 – The Silent Opening of Stillness & the Brotherhood of Youth

25 – The Deep Unspoken CORE Oath to Protect as Brothers & Fathers; for Our
Mothers and Kids

26 – Honor's Oration – LET MY WORD BE SAID – In Love

27 – OVER MORAL VIEW of Innocence Search for Who AM I

28 – Night Stalker – Polly's Lament

29 – 1965 – California Here We Come

30 – 1965 – My Father's Amend Buys My Trust

31 – 1966 – My Normality Disguise

32 – 1966 – Feeding My Hunting for Dissolution

33 – 1966 – Back to MSU via a Drunk or TWO

34 – 1967 – Hotel Restaurant School – And a License to Fun

35 – 1967 – HRI School Award – Streets of San Francisco

36 – 1967 – Friendly Ice Cream Hides Unconscious Derision

37 – 1967 – My Consumptions Echo the Arriving 70s

38 – 1968 – Domino's Pizza – My Career Begins to Lie and Forget

39 – 1969 – Our Family Starts Our Franchise

40 – 1970 – My INTERNAL CONFLICT With Men

41 – 70's The Rut of the Male FOR the Women Who Preen

42 – 1971 – My Own Night Club in Phoenix, Arizona

43 – 1972 – Sky Valley Ranch & Out the Back Door

44 – 1973 – The Boys; Our Last Run Hard; Till My Moody God; in Silence, Calls Me to the Mountains

45 – 70s OVERVIEW

46 – Allowing My Voice to BE

47 – My Heart In the Matter From the Wound of Love

48 – Drifting into the Story of The Deep Opening

49 – 1976 – Redwood City, EST and My Dad, et. al

50 – 1981 – The Approach to the Guru

51 – Adi Da Initiation of Release into my Vocal Serious Social Communication Destiny

52 – 1987 – Critical Moments BEFORE the First Drink

53 – 1997 – REHAB – Suicide or God – Show Me a Sign – NOW

54 – The Rapture of My Free Rendering of Sharing

55 – 1997 – Into the Fire My PENNANCE

56 – 1998 to 2000: ON the Bottom and Digging

57 – 2001 – My Work Begins

58 – The Initial Signs of Sobriety – OTHERS WANT YOU AROUND

59 – 2001 – Recovery Begins: November 11, 2006, The Miracle Happened for Me

INTRODUCTION

Alcoholism is a Disease

Alcoholism is a disease...Those that have this disease are just as sick as if they had cancer as if they had emphysema as if they had a heart condition...And they do have a condition of their own heart, But their feelings have been shut down...They have been abandoned from their feelings For others...they have anesthetized their ability to see others....they've coped with pains in their own experience, where the alcohol shuts down the ability to perceive right from wrong...Alcohol shuts down the ability to see others. Alcohol shuts down the ability to feel and to comprehend that your behavior is hurting other people...After a while the alcoholics behavior is unnoticeable by himself...he's usually coping with the blood sugar disease of alcohol of having to keep the pain of his own degeneration at bay by continuing to drink...And so the cycle of the alcoholic.

Those of us who have recovered and those of us who understand the disease realize the best thing we can do is to get involved in support programs: Al-Anon is one of the very best programs a nonalcoholic can use to cope with the partner that is in denial of the disease

...And this is especially true once the alcoholic partner has left the capacity for understanding your own condition is best dealt with in group along with personal counseling...

The person who HAS suffered the alcoholic, has been damaged, has had their ability to feel shutdown: they need to spend the time to recover their own sensibilities...and they need to turn away from the story of the alcoholic "that did it to them"…and they need to move on; into their own healing understanding…that they have work to do on themselves.

Emotional and psychological pain of betrayal is very difficult to transcend by one's self.

...Amends are intended to free the perpetrator from an event that the perpetrator now feels remorse and a sense of shame and has a definite understanding that whatever behavior had going on, there now resides a barrier, a mass of feelings, a combination of conflicts of feelings, all combining to suppress one's well-being...and now the burden is Undeniable and must be dealt with.

My mom & dad loved the outdoors: Fishing in Florida in the winter
Hunting Pheasant, Deer, Geese in Michigan in the fall :
To Be Outdoors & Share w/others or Alone with God – A Must

Finding Responsible Freedom, with Honor in: The Messages of Alcoholism

Alcoholism, for me, is now/was then an event, a motion of life's deeper expression of its responsible freedom.

Nothing in my childhood could express that.

But there's rawness in the rooms of alcoholics, drunk or sober. There's an innocence to be real that is the same drunk or sober, distinct from mentally disturbed.

Somehow, and some of, and many of, and most of in my experience, those who drink recognize their freedom unexpressed, so they shut down that doubt with glass of stout, so their true heart can be undressed.

You know, this wonderful play that we have with words, to think the song is the message. It's the listener's guidepost; it's visions of its wholeness that speaks to it from a plateau of certainty, you have a ways to climb—yes, I hold you dear, belay on my heart, travel up here, it is safe.

I await your presence. I make available the sacred space for your arrival. I will prepare myself for your expressions, so that I, as the listener, may disappear and dissolve into our mutual bonding; for without each other, who would listen, who would speak, and what would be said?

Miami Beach, Fla.
FEB 1941

Miami Beach, Fla.
FEB 1941

My mom raised as a happy orphan caring for babies. Adopted @ 7 Christian Science Minister; she demonstrated a gift of compassion.

My Father was a criminal attorney in Detroit , my Mother worked for Sally Rand, on staff: as burlesque dancer, actress eventually staff manager for New York and Chicago engagements.

She was Always A BEST FRIEND

My Mom — a Sponsor

About my mom: You probably know there's no way I could criticize that woman. Right ?

. . .God, no way.

Not only for how she behaved and what she taught me, but how she got through the Depression – you know, the economic depression – survived through the thirties and got a hold of my dad and then got sober in 1946.

You see, that's a life with no agreement. My mother wasn't asking for – and she couldn't receive – agreement. There's no mother and no father, so no voting.

And that was her freedom – that freedom because of the intensity and passion for her to survive; she passed down her instincts about what was real when you looked out at life and you looked out at people and told the truth about their behavior.

Now, I'm telling you this with a smile on my face.

I'm telling you this because both my parents were in a place about the humor about sexuality that I now find extremely humorous, but as a young boy was annoying.

Now, I won't tell you the really, really funny stuff – which I could tell you the really, really funny stuff. But here's a great story my mother told me.

Because my mom said there were often times when she was alone; she just had my sister in those years.

Now there wasn't anything about her life of drinking that was like, "I was alone with your sister and drunk," never!

That wasn't her drunkenness. My sisters had to drag her out of bars a few times; it would piss my sister off and she didn't like that. But my mother wasn't a fall-down drunk, she was a stand-up, good-looking woman who took care of business and I have compassion for that.

I can't help but to laugh. I feel like my mother's tickling me. It's ridiculous; you just had to know my mother. She's just, like, rolling; can't wait for me to tell you this. It's like, just back up. Back up.

Oh, you guys. You know, I've got some…I have some video of her. In iMemories – I'll make sure that you all see those.

Evelyn Charyl Burr: in the nineteen thirties; actually, right in the early thirties; 1931 –
1935. .. She had my sister when she was 17, 16…in 1928, right there, right?

So now she's gonna hit 19 in 1930 with three-year-old. Boom! Not a good place to be – on the streets of Chicago with no income. Boom! And, very attractive. . . .Ba-boom . . . Ka-Ching!

All right, I'll say it. She knew how to survive and she said this to me; but it never clicked . . . Oh, my god, I'm just too happy to say it.

She said to me, "Honey, when men would take me out, a lot of times when it was really difficult for me and your sister – and you'll understand this later in life, so I want you to hear it from me now, darling – When men would take me out, sometimes I knew they were gonna spend a lot of money on me, and I said to them, and I'd look them in the eye and I'd say, 'Look, whatever you're gonna spend for that fancy dinner, I'd rather you just give me that for me and my daughter and lets you and I just go out and party and have fun.'"

And you know—duh—and that's my mother, upfront.

Embarrassed? No, my mother was never embarrassed.

Those were two things; I said, "Mom, you don't seem to get embarrassed or depressed." She said, "Honey, I don't have time."

And that was it. That was my mom.

She kind of had a sense that was a little bit of an indulgence, in waiting for somebody to fix you, you know?

She didn't have time.

And we were into the next event; we were in the livingness of my relationship with my mom so that my life was, you know, protected by a woman who knew where her bread was and how it was buttered.

And she knew why she did what she did, and she knew why she did it and for whom. It was for me, and it was for my sister.

Eventually, it was for my father.

She good-wifed him; treated him with respect, made sure his meals were prepared, his laundry was washed – shirts were done professionally and ready in his drawer.

My father never had more than two days' worth of dirty laundry, I promise you. I watched my mother on the mangle – in the basement, pressing my father's and my T-shirts and our socks. . . .and happy to do it!

She had a rhythm in her life of gettin' shit done. She didn't complain – she didn't have time!

She went for her girls, her babies. There she had time; there was no time with my mom with those girls.

Those babies of hers were loved. . . but they were responsibly loved with a question: "Are you still living in the place of wanting to be sober, darling?"

I saw my mom sit on the edge of the couch many times with weeping women. It seemed boring sometimes because I – I'd fall back like sitting in the seat of a theatre...when we had to get over to that lady's house fast, she was in trouble—especially if a child was involved; and there I found friends, who hurt and needed play away...the glass was still on the table...my mom told me..." Take it away, to pour it in the sink".

Then...I'd sit back...and listen ...and watch my mom...just like my dad. But, she'd hold the women's hands and she talked to them and she'd allow them to cry but she wouldn't let them indulge.

She kept bringing them back to the point of:

..."what is the message to you here, darling?

What are you gonna do?

Look at me now, come on, look up.

I know you're sad, I know you've got things to talk about; but what do you want to do? What do you want to do right now?"

She'd be into the moment....!!!...because they couldn't...they were already
THERE – ready:...and they didn't know it.

. . but as soon as she got their attention and their eyes raised. She was there with a question:..."what do you want to do?"

And; they'd say...they wanted "to get sober".

So she'd ask them The First Step: "darling, are you powerless over alcohol? Is your life unmanageable?" and in that moment,....mmmmm; .... you know, The First Step ...is enough !

In the real, real moment of choosing recovery...for the novice, The First Step is way big.

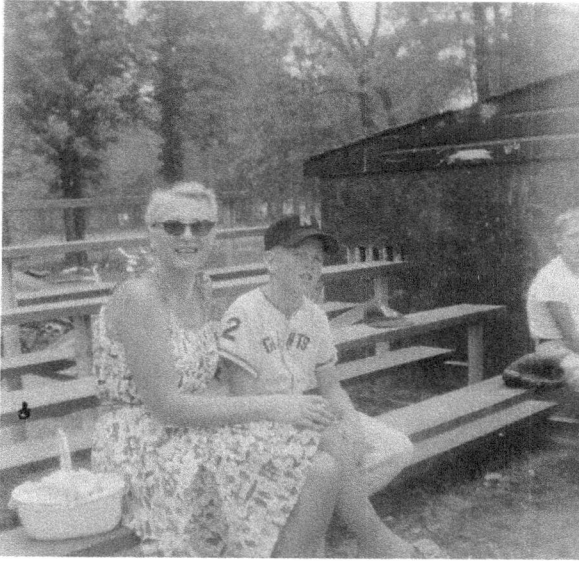

My mom came to ALL of my games
She made my life EASY & LOVED TO BE with me

It takes a big heart to be slow enough for an individual at the edge of suicide by their own hands, to choose to reach out and take the hand of another; in their own confession; in their own embarrassment and survive. You know?

I saw my mom do a lot of First Steps with folks.

I saw my mother do the first step with my friend, Warren's mother about eight times. I'm serious. It was horrible. It was hard on him; it was hard on his dad.

She might have twelve months and then boom; three months, boom; six months, boom- boom; six weeks, boom...a week, boom.

You never knew.

Everybody's attention was shook for days.

I got a chance to ignore it because I had seen the ones who were willing. And in her unwillingness, this arrogance that I'd seen is there in the insanity.

As a person who cares for others, you just give up.

It's like, Jesus, she doesn't care, she doesn't get it, and she doesn't want it. It's all right. Here, kitty, kitty, kitty.

I'd rather go to something that's loving, that wants attention.

So for my mom and me and my dad, you know, we're on fucking suicide watch with her. Nobody said anything but we're on suicide watch with her. He was my best friend, man. We slept together as friends. We were true brothers – still are.

But the nightmare that he had to put up with, poor soul, his mother constantly dipping into the bottle – both the liquid kind and the pills; and then there are no eating habits; she was a cripple so she couldn't get exercise.

Just one thing after another; and the nervous system just takes a dump...because there's no nutrition coming in.

People are in la-la land: "Gee, I don't know why my mom's so depressed, she hasn't eaten in four days, I'm kinda worried about her."

Well fuck, she's depressed because she hasn't eaten in four days. Wake up!

Damn: It is like I'm in the movie Moonstruck; I feel like I'm there with Cher and
Nicholas Cage; ...I feel like I'm slapping people in the face. ...Wake up!

It's that way.

And it isn't like spiritually wake up....it's...

SEE:...this is the lecture that does not fucking work for anyone to tell them what is wrong and what to do and not do.

That's just me here; stuck on my own petard...I got it up my ass...see it's just me here ...with this shaming & BLAMING.... That's ridiculous. It does not serve.

So getting back to the story of the breakdown: ...people have a ka-chunk for them, a Ka-Ching for them. some have a different kind of hard-on for life for them...that gets them TURNED ON but is not functional . . . IT is VERY Dysfunctional and mentally disturbed.

Get the intention of not throwing your life away with the good ideas and what never happened.

Get rid of the bad thoughts of who didn't shame you.

It's all the reverse of what people think and it's all backed up because nobody digs and says, "I'm not clear; I'm not present; I'm not Whole; I'm not Complete. Thanks for asking."

And I'm not certain that even this monologue is gonna get that question to even show up for folks.

Right now, my intention is just to cut it loose here in my tale...to let people get a feeling that everybody's got a voice and a rhythm when they're sober. You got a swagger when you're sober. You find out shit about yourself when you're sober you just can't see when you're drunk and using out of control. You can't.

There's these wonderful, joyful ways that you want to eat life that are not on the plate at Denny's, or even at John Ash or whatever fancy restaurant you want to go to; it's not there.

It's the opening in your own self and the morning to the adventure of what's up and the joy of let's do it. With the capacity to let's share it. And the assurance others will be there to share the experience with you. And that's being on purpose. And that's what we want.

That's the true message here: Once the freedom of sanity is ensured in your own cleansing; ...life will show up and take you away.

The hard part is getting it all cleaned up through the steps....one at a time.

Spring 1953 – My Final Piano Recital – yr 3
I played : Moonlight Sonata 1st Movement

My Dad—a Sponsor

Yeah, about my dad. You know, I don't even know where to start with him. He was invisible to me. He was me. He was the big me. There was never a sense of separation really between he and I, for I saw his world through his eyes. I was made all right, I was made safe.

He was the alpha male for our family and for hundreds of underprivileged people as a defense attorney. He was the kind of individual who had compassion for people, who could ecstatically stand in that wound after losing his own father at 12 years old who he was dearly close to. It left him, a boy of 13, fatherless.
His mother was--a huge heart, my grandmother. She just finished having this fifth baby. There they are in 1918. His father died after going back to the war a second time after being wounded – re-

commissioned and sent back. He was killed. His body's still there in France.

You know, a 13-year old boy and his mom with four kids, and he's the oldest--very difficult. Although they didn't have to want, for my grandfather left them an estate and was bought out by his real estate partners. My grandmother was blessed that way; my grandfather made certain that if anything were to happen to him that they would never have to work. My grandmother never had to work ever--praise God.

My father was raised in that period down there in downtown Detroit, Harrison Avenue near the river. Things got tough during the mid-'20s. Good buddies of his, the Bernstein's from--guys like to row across that river and get the alcohol from Windsor and bring it back. Those were school chums of his, and they ended up calling those boys, "the purple gang." So those guys and my dad had fun getting them in and out of jail. The money was flowing. You know, you've got the '20s.

So my dad, born in 1906; 1926, my dad's 20 years old. He's also an attorney for the Moriarity Law Firm, and he's a defense attorney. He's draw to that event because a part of him likes to play on that rough side and the tough side. And he drank hard and he lived hard and he lived clean and he lived well. My grandmother expected him to use his funds to keep himself immaculate, which he did. He always dressed to the nines. He was very well behaved, extremely sharp table manners.

Everything was very formal at my grandmother's house. Each one of grandchildren had our own napkin rings every Sunday. They were made out of silver. Two plates in front of us--that was special Sunday dinner. Grandmother sat at the front of that table, and she managed the table with authority and grace; and conditioned the room, and everyone that was in it, that we were in the presence of God at all times. Again, the divine is blessing of the food, and we're extremely grateful.
His Son stands with us individually and walks with us individually. As incomprehensible as that can be, a single unified entity called Jesus Christ is individually assigned to us by the Creator. So fear not, you will always be given the right choices.

Your job is to tell the truth about what you see.

First, to yourself, before you make the choice.

I'm done with the metaphors and concepts in speaking and all the time and energy they suck up....and...by the way, I forgave him — my dad — it wasn't his fault.

But then, to an 8-year-old boy, after the unnecessary extensive part to these violent beatings, when that part of him went dormant; he replaced those moments with his assurance of his love for me - yet; I knew there was a place in him that was still there, I would see it...and I wasn't foolish enough to abstract myself from the high watch of surviving his betrayal to be involved in playing with any four letter word or to tell anyone…what I felt...no one knew — not my mom — no one — and yet maybe, because he only did this to me three times and all the time afterward he'd assure me he loved me, as he held me close — yet, it was always true — I still could feel and depend on his love and care for me all my life — our life together — I loved him happily until his death — and now I see, by grace, we both were spared the memory of the horror of his discipline breaking my trust — I remembered it all in a workshop, in my 30s, after he died .

The incident was the Saturday before a friend of mine — my best friend, Warren, we were eight and this is in the summer of '52. Warren and I had gone next door to our neighbors, who were the Terranova's, and they had just moved from Italy. They had this incredible garden, including 6' tall tomato plants with just, you know, dozens and dozens of tomatoes. Now, to two 8-year-old boys with nothing else left to do, those things splatter really cool up against the side of a garage — you ever noticed? If you get the ones that are a little softer — oh, man, they make a huge splat — you ought to see it, it's really fun.

So the next morning, my father comes into my bedroom.

This memory is as clear as any memory I've ever had. I can tell you what he was wearing. I can tell you what the colors of my sheets were. I can tell you how my pajamas felt on me as I slid them off me, because that's the first time he'd ever asked me to do that.

He came in my room, and it was early — it was a Sunday morning, normally we get up and go to church. So he came in and said, "Bruce." I was groggy, and I said, "Yes." He says, "Wake up." And I kind of turned, and I was on elbow. He says, "I want you to wake up now, son." I said, "What?" He said, "I need to ask you some questions." I said, "Okay."

You gotta remember, my dad's a trial attorney. This guy came from the interesting part of Detroit during the time when the Purple Gang were school chums of his, but he was on the other side of that ticket, and made some extra money with the Moriarty Law Firm getting those boys out of jail. So my dad knew how to play it rough and he knew how to play it tough, and he knew what was right and he knew what was wrong. He was about six years sober, been working the program. I'd seen him doing that for a long time.

Good man.

I'd never seen him really angry. There was a force in him — he was a barrel-chested, very well structured upper body, about 5'8", 180 lbs. He was like his dad; they were kind of like big, thick forearms, hands and chest, little legs — kind of funny. I got my mom's legs and my dad's upper body, so I got the best of both those folks. I got the best of both those folks in many different ways.

This was a moment that was about to imprint on me a permanent condition — that's why I'm talking about this this way. As I told you I would, I would slow things down, so as to allow more of the essence, you know, of the experience. I've never talked about that moment before — pulling into Barnes & Noble talking about, you know, a moment where what could be considered abuse today, became a foundation for an intelligence now that I believe I was initiated at that point; an intelligence that says, I know where the edge of death is, so nothing else matters.

So when he came in, he asked me, "Were you over at the Terranova's yesterday?" I said, "Yeah." He said, "Did you smash those tomatoes up against the garage?" I said, "Yeah." He said, "How many?" I said, "Oh, maybe 12." He said, "Do you realize that that was food for those people?" I said, "No." He said, "Did

you understand that you went in and damaged people's property?"
"No."

"Son, I want you to take your pajama bottoms off. I'm going to take my belt off, and I'm going to hit you 12 times, and at the end of every time I hit you, I'm going to ask you if you'd do it again—do you understand?"

In that moment, everything was starting—my body was starting to get this intense prickling nervous. I remember getting my thumbs and sliding into the band of my pajamas and slid them down. I remember the belt coming out of the belt loops, and I watched his hand double it up, held the buckle in his hand, it was just the end of the strap, the loop. His shirt sleeves were already rolled up. I looked at his face, and he had this—you know how the mouth is kind of tightened up with an intensity of commitment?

He said, "Lay down." and I said, "No, no, no, Daddy." He says, "Lay down." And that's when it started. I don't want to take you any deeper.

Suffice it to say, it took approximately three minutes/4 minutes for him to finish the 12th. Somewhere, I believe around the 8th, there was a peace that just took over, because he was taking his time. He would ask me, are you going to do it again—9, 8, 7, 6—somewhere around 5, I don't remember anything else.

I didn't get out of bed that day. My mother came up and tried to read me our favorite book together, *The Wizard of Oz*. I wasn't very interested. There was like—my tongue was feeling swollen. When my mom first started to talk to me, her voice was, like, far away.

I hold no harm now, for I see his intention was in making me aware of who I could trust and what to look for when I did and what is real is love and what isn't—that is what I learned.

Through all of my lessons of life as my Spiritual growth I have not "learned" I am Divine Spirit or have I "earned" the right to say that I am the Divine Itself because I my spent time looking for God—the already existing Divine self of my life.

These culminating life experiences have just allowed me to consciously release any abstractions of my attention from my whole, complete and Divinely blessed Presence; to be alive and well as all I simply am aware of...I have no more movement left in me to move from my bliss and assign blame or even hold on to any regret as to my person.

I forgive – I forgive – I forgive.

My father is well, and his training of me as and is now understood as perfect. I accept all of my personal history as what is so and receive my own gifts of Divine Presence by turning to people like you reading this opening you have created in me to remove the final thought that my dad was mean by any intention or predator like stalked design.

He was a beautiful loving man—he loved his mother, me, my mother and all of my many relatives deeply and actively. He showed me what it looked like to care for others in crisis. I have his AA chip dated 12/8/1946 LD (last drink). He was my friend and would talk to me about how he saw life. I watched him and my mom go to AA meetings all his life. They started five Michigan groups and two in Canada. I attended hundreds of meetings with them from the time I was two till I was a mature teen. I watched my father reach out to people on the street; stop them, talk to them face to face and usually would give them money. There were moments when he brought home alcoholic men; who'd spend hours with my dad confessing their stories, until somehow my dad would look deeply into their eyes and ask a very slow and deliberate question—then the crying began and sometimes tears fell on our kitchen table...I sat there, open eyed, felt these men...listened to their "new felt honesty" of talking with my dad, his real use of words, showing and sharing his meanings of fear and love while healing another.

So, I do these essays—this is a purge here. I've never allowed THAT moment to really be fully felt, in anyone's company. And today, I realize that this intelligence now that I own and the abstractions to which I communicate to you from, was initiated that day, and it's always been here. I've always been curious why, when I put my attention on something, I just really figure it out quickly.

But the one thing I could never figure out is why anyone would be covertly hostile with me, or passive/aggressive, especially if they said they were in my tribe. You know, that part of becoming wise now has taken its seat. I don't expect everyone to hear me, and I expect some people to betray themselves.

Oh, the other thing I just remembered…My dad never touched me before or after those incidents when I was 8, in any aggressive or violent way—ever.

My father never made a demand on me to be any way, or do anything, that just was not true of me—ever.

He showed me what it was like to feel and weep for another openly…To be there with his whole Being to allow forgiveness to felt by all.

And only by Divine Grace again: Now, thirty years after his death, I had not had any real memories of him since his death:

Now…I am now flooded with these memories of my life with my dad…with deeper re-awakenings with unexpected healings for me to feel, remember and to finally acknowledge these conscious choices—that demonstrated the love and the wisdom of my father.

THE CHILDREN – That's What This is All About

In the face of knowing and accepting, I'm a poet; in the face of knowing, accepting that I'm an author; in the face of knowing that my words spill out of my heart and my soul, and rhyme and reason to no one else but myself, I allow this power of speech to be — I don't hide from it at all, I can't, there's nothing left.

It's the children I think of, you must understand.

Enjoy as you will, but pass it on, please.

This is the message — I shall hang this story upon this word:

We have a responsibility to shine back…Before they enter the rooms of the parties of adolescent…We get to shine back to the children, the consequences of their choices;…We get to shine back to the children, so that they see and can tell us what they see before they enter that room and make that choice to have fun, and to remember to leave the room.

So, in this profound statement of accountability, to all of us who listen to this accounting remember:

It's not about me — it's not about you — it's about the children.

That's…What THIS…is all about.

PROLOGUE — An Offering of My Selfish Gift

As I feel this grace in this performance, this singular performance, I feel you guys so much.

It's important to pause here just for a sec.

Because you can hear, it's the voice of any person.

It's the moment of any person; and it's that beyond the drinking to the place of the stillness undisturbed alive, intelligent, and safe and innocent.

Knowing it's simply here...just simply here.

That confession: the place where I reside in that discovering of those confessions. It is holy, it feels so holy, in a way because of the innocence that's being revealed of us all, the ability to be helpless and the motion of a good person, but to be helpless — that's exactly where we are.

But we don't reside there, see; we don't sit there; we don't allow there to be there — we dance around there; we entertain there, we overeat there; and we forget there, we are there always here.

So that time for me is this time for me, this pause for me.

I wanted to reopen up the core, what the intention is, of anyone who sits down and writes, and allows the voice of experience to speak.

Somehow in this wonderful theater, the song of the soul sings so simply, I can't help but let it say itself — it's too obvious. It takes over, but it's not a distance any one of us is from; it's in the core, out of the core, it's nowhere away from.

See, that's the revealing, as our innocent stillness and our intelligence and our strength. And to honor that as I am; the place, the Beingness, as our wholeness; we then thoroughly get to enjoy the theater of the present listening to someone else's performance.

We must honor the listener, and we must open up the ears deeper and wider to recognize the authentic source of all — of all of all. l'Chaim — there's no other way to say it.

And it is that, and this is that.

Oh, the few ears that shall enjoy this song.

Yes, tears will fall for all of us, you see.

The simplicity of moving waves of love — it's all this is to you guys.

As I sit here in the blooming wine orchards, sitting in the sunshine, and the passing trucks, and people on the way to their lives — always available for a glance, though, you know.

In that instant, this instant, the profundity of who we are is revealed. And I hope, and I pray, and I suggest, and I say this — this part is all for you.

NOW IT BEGINS — The Gift of Your Listening to Me for ME

The clarity now for me of my own independence — as what I hear and see and say — is profoundly obvious I am that — and in your company. I certainly have demonstrated that I am that most profoundly.

So, for me, is having the responsibility now to relax into that, as opposed to muscle it forth.

It's a different form of a battle. It's the urge to war with resolve to sit down, and trust that peace will arrive, and that it's on its way, and it's of not my concern, but to respond — for, I can trust my instincts now.

The sense of being abstracted couldn't be further than the truth for me. Most demonstrated in the fact that my two primary relationships — my ex-wife and my current wife, are very dear and close to me, and each one have a very powerful relationship with me that's supportive for everyone.

There became clear today, to me, in a declaration — not a declaration so much — my independence from them. But my resolve to have them see my independence as my own wholeness, complete whole, nothing needs to happen; and from that place, I declared that I could distinguish the difference between them and me, and they saw that. It just was a moment, and I stood — and as I do. But the soliloquy of the announcement of my independence was even profound to my ears — for it wasn't about the commitment to a belief of something greater than what was so, it was the already truth of the living condition of this intelligent innocent presence that sees clearly and speaks clearly now.

To say it's myself would be inappropriate. It's an expression of what I am in words — so I move forth now. You know, you're my devoted listeners here, and I am authentically just fallen in the heart with the matter.

There's a continuation of this blessing of the celebration of my independence, and it just has to be acknowledged — that's the message here; that as much as I could say that there's a great conclusion, the truth is that there's just this breathing opening, and conscious resolve to respond with intelligent kindness.

OUR CONTRITION: BE A Confessional; BE the Heart of Listening

As many principles in the relation to our awareness and our presence, confession is good for the soul, you know. It isn't just a confession like a repeated story. When the confession is truly expressed, or a withhold is truly expressed, or an anger is truly expressed, or a resentment is truly expressed, or forgiveness is truly expressed — there's a disappearance of what was before, and the beautiful healing power of the word removes the mental obstruction, creates what's called a mental equivalent and disappears the event to the experience, so that the individual rests free in the magic of its own word.

These principles — these are the things that we are universal. It's not a conversation, it's demonstrateable that our word causes and creates and acknowledges where life sits, and what it says, and how it looks from the point of view of the Being who's having the experience of life over there.

You know, again, I get ready to fall in this rapture. It's like a lecture of love. It's like I resist doing it; it's like a lecture of love. I can't keep it back, you know, it takes over my breathing and the pattern of thought, and it allays it for me, and breathes me and tickles me, and says it's all right — it's always perfect, always perfect.

That unbelievable event of reality is so incomprehensible to us, so we consider ourselves separate and un-whole.

The magic of our word that says that we're whole in the event of our declaration — frees our soul.

So, these words are not meant to entangle one's heart, in a cipher of words, that appear to release...It's just a simple confession of where one stands. It's nothing more than that.

Yet, the true release comes in the knowing that the audience listens, at the level of fullness, so there's no question about the reception of the communication...which comes unguarded, and falls from the mouth as a relief, and is received by the other as a gift, and released in the fullness of knowing that the other has shared something that was hidden and undisclosed. That sharing brings the light of consciousness and the light of healing to that individual, to which they walk cleaner in that area of their own becoming.

They don't have to fear what it is that they've said, in those words that they feared.

The confession of the feeling of the emotion in the entanglements of the words, no matter if they made sense at all, is the motion of the intention of the heart to free itself. It isn't even in the connecting of any dots of paragraphs and meaning. The listener's heart, the listener's love, and the listener's compassion is what the speaker is looking for, and the speaker falls into that event and it's mindless — like Mom — always there, always forgiving, always gentle, and reminding you you're not alone.

SATURDAY : January 7, 2012 11:20am

<u>WHERE TO START</u>

When I look at where to start, the tendency is always to chronologically jump into something, you know?

We have the respect for one another to try to tell one another things in order.

So the apparent sequence can be shared as a completion and another can choose to listen and hear and take what they like and leave the rest. And the space of feeling complete is there.

But sometimes in the listening...the chronological event doesn't bring forth the impact.

Especially when one wishes to speak from the middle of the bottom.

But being an alcoholic, chronology is always an excuse: "It happened to me back there...Sit down, let me tell you how my luck was so bad...If you only understood, they did it to me...Yeah, IF she only didn't betray me...Like I had to do it afterwards, just to get even...But I didn't like her anyway...But after I woke up in bed with her, that morning...and didn't know who she was...and going home to my wife...and kinda feeling like, ok, so she fucked another guy, so what..!"

...So let's go on: the middle of that bottom!

...It's a bottom of no reflection...

…Because it's the bottom...

...And it's just an expression...

…BUT it's the bottom...It's motionless, it has its head down...

…Head down . .!!!

That's how I got how to start this…

Sitting here in the parking lot what we in Michigan called Party Stores.

We LOVE party stores. We do. We love party stores, they're a blast; they're party stores.

"Yo! It's Friday! TGIF! Man,"…We'd just get the six-pack in by eleven before we'd head to the bar…

Party stores are awesome, man!

God, when we were young bucks running around, didn't have any money, Friday afternoon, all you'd have to do is get close to those party stores…and when the frat boys hit it…we'd come in right behind 'em…we look like just one of the same frat boys just laid out $400 to buy eighteen cases of beer…Except when they got back, there were only fourteen.

We always got our beer on Fridays. You get real clever when you're an alcoholic and you're broke.

But that's not an alcoholic, is it? No, it isn't.

It's just life there—adolescent life there, unexpected life there…familiar life there…perfect life there…dangerous life there…

So as I sit here…trying to look at where to begin. I put my head on the steering wheel here…

…Then I remembered every time I put my head on a steering wheel and the alcohol wouldn't work anymore…I knew if I kept drinking, I'd finally fall asleep.

But there are times outside that party store…where there's nowhere to go…

And sometimes outside that party store…sometimes…but…but not for me...

...But for my sponsor, Jimmy. Jimmy G!

That's where he was! He had his head down! ...At a party store...!

...The heroin....

...The crack cocaine....

...The vodka....

...Twenty grand...

...And it wasn't going to be enough...!

AA SUNDAY MIXED BOWLING LEGUE — Motor City Lanes (Connor and Mack) 1950s & 60s.... My mom best 265 & dad best 287 carried over 200 averages at one time...this woman could bowl.

ONE

I Want to be an Alcoholic When I Grow Up...

"When I grow up, I'm going to become an alcoholic, so I can join AA."

That's what I said when I was three years old.

My mom used to kid about it, but that was my love commitment to Jimmy Murtaugh, alcoholic.

Those were almost the first few words I said when I was 2. God, except for the pipe smell — which, I loved the pipe; he was this jolly love-bucket, and he was one of my father's sponsees.

And in that environment—in innocence, of recovering alcoholics—I felt the heart of the matter. I knew through sincerity, without it speaking to me, that we were all equal…Because we were all present, and because only one of us spoke at a time in the kitchens, the living rooms, the dining rooms at my parents'. The respect is in the audience. No cross-talk. There was the openness and the sincerity to understand and to be with the speaker; for unless they were telling a joke or sharing a new, fun experience in life, they had just fallen into a confession, and we became their confessors.

Nobody thought about it: AA meeting in the home; in a building; in a car; on a street.

It's caused in the listening, in the certainty by the speaker, that the vulnerability of their now-awakened heart sees a distinction that they must confess; for they see that they haven't fully made amends to their own innocence…And somehow were just kind of lying about the past, and they wanted to forgive themselves. They wanted to share that insight.

And in the completion of that share, there wasn't applause, there wasn't a clap, there wasn't a thank-you, Bill, there wasn't a "Who's next in this meeting?"

There was a gentle merging into the motion of passing the salt, or my mother saying thank-you.

And then life moved on. For in the chapel home of my parents, that natural innocence that was rebirthing itself at 30 and 40 years old was my friend and was me—innocent among them, knowing nothing. And yet, having a trail of pain, an illusion of separateness, that the sharing of which was intrinsic and endemic to the healing of everyone, for the pain always seen upon the face couldn't be denied.

And when that pain showed up upon the face, the people spoke and they spoke, because they knew their pain was seen upon their face, and they gave it up without thinking. Because the space was about relieving the face from the separation of its own joy in the body, in the heart and the soul of the confessor, my friends.

TWO

My First Sights of Living Alcoholics & Their Consistent Behavior

My first view of alcohol's dysfunction was in my uncle, my mother's brother.

What an interesting man, Jack Burr. He was a genius — so my mother said — worked for Milton Bradley, was very involved in creating Monopoly, so the story goes.

He was a small man, 5'6" at best, thin, always…"off the bus."

But he was the one where I first really got the smell of and the look of the alcoholic in motion of itself.

The smell and the behavior were one. That's what I came to see, that anytime anyone smelled like that, they behaved like that — like my 5'6", 130 pound, dysfunctional genius uncle — incapable of driving, but interesting.

"And he's leaving when…?" would kind of be where I was at, because of the smell.

I do not believe he ever spent a night at our home.

I remember when he came and saw us, he was just reeking, and his clothes were those ill-fitting wide-collared…He dressed in a suit with the shoes, but everything was old and unclean, for me.

And that was the place from where I knew my parents had extracted their friends. From what appears to be the place that this man, my mother's brother, lived. She and he and her sister were all orphans by her mother, who was "an actress"; but she and her brothers and sisters never knew their father, and the birth certificate says "Baby Burr," and…That's about it. You know, no trail, no fathering.

So this man was really a classic example of unobstructed alcoholism and drinking to its death, to which he did.

I do not know anything about the details.

My mother was always very protective of me. She was the strongest female I ever knew. She was always stronger, faster, cleaner, dearer, more loving, hugging, on her toes, on her feet than any other woman I've ever known.

Her street smart, high-level intelligence kept the world around me safe, such that I just had my own experience guided by my own interests, which she shared for music and dance. She and I danced. God, we had a ball.

She came to every one of my baseball and football games. My father came to zero, so, you know.

That was just the way it was.

I was into my thing and my dad's not there. He loved me; many times I slept with him at night. I don't give a shit about him not being at the football game, but my mom was there to cheer me on, in her outrageous Lucille Ball voice. She was a combination — Lucille Ball and Madonna. I always felt it would take at least both of those women just to get started to even be sober.

And, I mean, that's kind of what I've come to see. She was dead-on, a conscious female taking care of her son.

My father was also a very intelligent man when sober.

Both sober in 1946: They both came off the street as survivors that were very successful in their own alcoholism, such that they knew the difference.

Once at AA, my mother gave my dad an ultimatum, such that with inside of one month, my dad was in the program.

She came in November 11, '46, and my dad was in on the 8th of December '46, and they never looked back.

It was a wonderful event of these individuals being freed from the complexities of the entrapments of the continual lying to oneself, covered up by the illnesses that can be contracted from the deep generation of the over-consumption of alcohol.

It is one thing to have lies and then to be playful. It's another to bet your life on those lies—a lot of alcoholics do, and they pay the price.

Fifteen percent recover who choose.

I'm exceptional, and I'm also driven, and I'm also inspired as you can well tell.

It's not about the disease of alcoholism. It's about the disassociation that we have with our own experience. It's the lack of validation of our own good nature and good sense. Getting that grounded first, so that it's common, like common sense.

So, my uncle was the antithesis of the unrecovered alcoholic, even though he was directly in the line of the option to choose to recover.

The other smelly part of alcohol for me was Frank Domachowski, who was a carpenter, a wonderful guy. God, he was just a Jimmy Durante kind of guy, you know what I'm saying?

He was that good ah-cha-cha kind of Polish carpenter who had a wife, but just could not stay out of the sauce, and he got dysfunctional and angry. It's usually these guys that ended up in our basement, or the guys that dad said, you have an option. When they cried on the table after my dad brought them home, they had some conditions to meet. And to the level they could or could not take care of themselves, if they were willing to recover, my father would take care of the rest.

He only wanted them to choose to recover. He didn't expect them to be perfect. We all know that that isn't what occurs.

The process of continuing to choose is a combination of a capacity of someone asking, in the space of the question do you want to recover? That's not an easy question to just say, "Yes!"

It has to be proposed at the right time where the individual is really capable of seeing the distinction of his behavior — unobstructed drinking and the destiny. When someone is in the midst of a day after, the night before…that is a good time to ask.

Because folks are available because they are feeling like, "Holy shit, what train just hit me?"

 Yeah, do you want to do it again?

That's the wonderful process that is open to all of us, in the process of allowing others around us to recover from anything.

Is this working? Do you want to change? Is there anything I can do to help you?

That's pretty much it. And that's all this adventure's going to be about.

Because only those that have gotten this far are going to be into either into the adventure of the recovered alcoholic, or there's a contiguous listening that breaches and reaches out from the cartoon of the story to the reality around us and you, to who's not sober.

So it's just not a lay-down here of the chronology of the ride of the beast.

This is another moment. This is another opportunity. This is another message: That choice is the way out.

And sometimes others don't know there's a choice. If we see that, we have to ask them, "Hey, how's it going? Would you like it to be different, or would you like it to remain the same?"

THREE

Frank D — Our Live-in Alcoholic Carpenter

I want to talk about Frank Domachowski.

He was quite an influence to me in regards to the observation of the individual who was struggling with the condition of alcoholism. Frank lived in our basement on Littlestone Road in Grosse Pointe Woods.

My parents and I had moved from the Kean Apartments; downtown Detroit on Jefferson Avenue around 1949, and they had just built these homes in Grosse Pointe Woods. The neighborhood hadn't been finished yet, and we were one of the homes on the street, now just a pattern — a crisscross pattern of 100,000 homes that now carpet that part of Detroit — Harper Woods and Grosse Pointe, along St. Claire Shores there, headed up to Sarnia and up to the thumb, and all along the whole Detroit River area.

We moved out there in 1949, and my house hadn't been finished, and the garage was yet to be built. The house next door, the ground hadn't even been broken yet.

I can remember the joy we all had and the adventure of going there, and all the unique hiding places and fun places that myself — who was raised in an apartment…This was exotic playground. It continued to be that way.

I grew up in the midst of the Grosse Pointe coming of age. Every piece of territory within a mile or two miles of that location, I knew on my bike. It was just too much fun to watch Grosse Pointe grow. Into my teenage years, I went out with friends and explored the Ford mansion, when it became vacated — it was down on Jefferson Avenue — exciting stuff like that for teenage boys.

Littlestone Road was a beautiful 3-bedroom home with a basement.

Frank Domachowski showed up as a function of his alcoholism. He was a sponsee of my father's, he was broken, he had nothing except incredible carpentry skills.

I spent more time around this man—helping him, being with him—while he was mostly sober. Of course, you could always tell when he'd been drinking—he couldn't hide it.

My dad never threw them out. It wasn't like that; he couldn't.

You understand, alcoholism is a biochemical, psycho-emotional disease of the lack of choosing the opportunity to be whole, because one's never known it.

I've personally been blessed with the experience of being conscious of alcoholism and felt personally whole from the time I was a child; with the oration of principles of AA and watching its dynamic. Yet, the emotional part of my own self that needed to experience and explore and go through those narrow passages and be delivered by God as a resurrection to the principles.

But that's a long way from a basement on Littlestone.

Frank Domachowski, for me, in the stories I'll share about him—he'll come in and out as we breeze through the times in my childhood when I take a look at the influences that alcohol had, in its positive and negative ways—represented the observing space of a growing young man.

Frank was so skilled and the basement was completely unfinished. The garage had not been done. I watched him and my father build this garage; in fact, I have a photograph of the two of them on top.

There was a fun part of the man that, when he was sober, there was a joy, there was a giving, there was a carefreeness about him. He always looked out for you in a simple way. He had all of his tools in this one handmade toolbox. He made all of his toolboxes.

One of the favorite things I had in my life was he made a toy box for me with "Bruce" on the side.

That was wonderful, you know…It was like a passageway into Narnia's adventures, because I kept everything in there: my football shoulder pads…the stuff I had as a kid, all the different things I tried on—my soldiers, helmet and guns, my cowboy guns; all the toys that I had—the teddy bears, and the games, and the balls, and the balls…and the balls. It was a large toy box. It was probably 24x36 on the bottom, and about 24x36 at the top, and a lid on it, so it closed.

That's what my mom liked, is, "Honey, put all your toys in the toy box"—down in the basement.

Frank Domachowski lived down there, stayed down there. But the times that he did drink were not good.

The times anybody drank around my father, I watched him behave in very, very straightforward, honest, calm…For it was a clearinghouse—our home—this place my father knew that he could contain the attention of the alcoholic.

So, the real sequence, you had to detox them. That's what we did with Frank.

There were times when I had to clean up his puke and wash his clothes, and just take care of the man. I was a kid. It's like taking care of a big dog—sick. They just love the shit out of you for it.

You get to have that privilege as a child: to be there in the moving illness, watching the eyes and the surrender that someone has, and the blink of "thank you, so glad you're here." That's ageless, timeless, and it doesn't matter how old you are.

I was privileged to recognize that glance in folks, and to become comfortable with the reception of that suffering, and to acknowledge, "You're welcome."

It's that kind of primal event in my own person that I want to honor in us. We're all Samaritans. We're all patients of our own suffering by the lack of choosing, and lack of understanding and knowing.

It's just more of a lack of the opportunity to have the distinction.

That's all it really is. Of course, in the life of Frank Domachowski, that kind of sophisticated talk would have gone way over his head; but we're not there. These stories that I blend and bring from the past must integrate into the consideration here. It must be a living event.

What was true then is true now.

And so these templates of healing are secure. The behavior is repetitive on all sides. Just like in the speaking, you create the listening. In the healing, there is the "to be" and the "want to be."

There's the difference.

FOUR

Tommy I — Demonstrates the Edge of the Question of Recovery

When I was about nine, my dad had a sponsee of his who'd been around for quite some time — Tommy Isles.

Tommy was a good, beautiful, Irish man; in fact, he's in the picture at my fourth birthday. He's the one sitting on the left; that beautiful sweet smile that he has. He's sitting next to Mae Morgan, who's looking at him; she's one of my mom's sponsees. My dad's there with his hands on his hips, smiling away. Jimmy Murtaugh took that picture. There's my dad's sponsor Bill Burke, who I've got my hand on, and his wife, Mary, my mother's sponsor... And my devoted loving mother.

Tommy Isles was always a devoted sober man, a devoted loving man, a man who had honor from the very first time I met him.

He's the only man I ever watched get into a fight and beat another man to his knees, with the potential of the knock-out punch. The clarity of the moment was, "Thou on your knees had best repent, for the next moment is in your hands."

That little bit of proverbial staging is around an incident that Tommy Isles demonstrated integrity for me, as it occurs with the blessing of my father.

Tommy had come over to our house and was talking with my father in the kitchen. They were talking, just sharing a moment together. The next moment, there was a knock on the side door, and one of my dad's new sponsees showed up drunk, stepped in the house. Tommy didn't say anything, was polite. My dad said, "Come on in," and opened up another seat at the kitchen table. I knew it was going to be one of those moments where maybe this guy was going to get it, or maybe he was going to go back out and drink some more. Everybody was kind of suspenseful and not really knowing what might happen in the very moment.

I was sitting in the far corner of the kitchen table and my dad had some coffee out, and I think I had a glass of milk, because I liked to listen. Tommy was sharing his life, I can't remember the details, but God, he was a happy guy. I loved his smile, and he was just bright—that's all I can tell you—he was just bright.

This guy comes in, Bill Harris, and when he comes in, he comes up and steps into the kitchen, steps up next to my dad, and my dad's kind of offering him a chair. He says to Tommy, "What the hell you doing here?" He says, "You're still a drunk."

I kind of froze, because this guy was angry, and we didn't ever have angry people in our home.

Tommy stood up like a guy and said, "Excuse you, you're in Stuart's home, you need to change your attitude right now—I don't care if you've been drinking."

The guy says, "Yeah? What are you going to do about it?"

My dad looked at Tommy, and he said, "Take it outside."

Tommy grabbed this guy by the collar. They were outside on the driveway.

Tommy pushed him back, said, "Okay, I'm going to ask you one more time. Do you understand what's going on here? Do you understand you're drunk, you're over at Stuart's home, and you insulted me?"

This guy was not getting the scene.

I'm upstairs—my dad said, "You—outta here." I couldn't come out on the driveway. I ran up the stairs and I was looking out through the window, which is over the top of the driveway, watching these two guys.

This guy comes right at Tommy, and Tommy just grabbed him by the collar and just slapped him silly, and then punched him and knocked him down—just punched him the face, and his nose was broken right there.

Then he grabbed him and said, "You need to apologize right now."

He said, "I apologize, I'm so sorry."

They then he came in the house.

I was privileged enough to be able to be called down to get the ice.

That was a long evening.

Bill Harris became Tommy's sponsee. That reality show didn't take long, because even Harris—when he showed up, he wanted it. He wanted the confrontation, to be smacked down, to get his nose broken. It wasn't that hard of a hit—his nose wasn't broken that bad.

And then, it was all done. When the coffee started, when the crying started, there was another person who showed up in Bill Harris. It was the one who wanted to show his drunkenness, his disrespect, his boyishness—for the last time. He wanted this time to be the last one. He wanted this group of men to witness it—that this incident, this young boy—that this is what the adjustment looks like.

Bill became a nice man, but we didn't see too much of him. We heard he went back out again. We saw him time to time in meetings, but the impression of who Tommy Isles was and the Hall of Justice that was created by my father were the law to behave, to be appropriate, to be available, to be honest, open, willing.

That stuff of the program is for children and for sane people, and Tommy Isles…

Tommy Isles was a beautiful man.

FIVE

The LIVES of the Liquid Alcohol, Beer, and Wine

There just wasn't any drinking in our family.

My grandmother, on Sunday, had a glass of sherry. She let me taste it and it tasted like rotten prune juice.

Then my grandfather, John Patterson—my step-grandfather—had a ritual. When he'd get home from work would have one or two Pabst Blue Ribbon beers sitting there in his chair with a bowl full of Planter's peanuts. That was every day, including Sunday, in the evenings. That was his ritual. I remember the bottle. I remember sitting in his lap, I remember him giving me and my cousins a taste—and it was like, oh, jeez, with the bubbles and just—horrible. He had one of these Pilsner glasses, you know, these long neck ones. He enjoyed it. I enjoyed watching him pour it, and it sat there: the picture of him there in his chair next to the fireplace with the end table and the lamp and the Pilsner glass and the peanuts: Grandpa.

He was a beautiful man and simple man and forward man…And alcohol—it was beer to me.

There was a huge distinction between the glass of sherry, the pilsner of beer, and dysfunctional alcoholics fighting or throwing up on my floor in the basement, and their angular behavior.

There was no statement in any kind of behavior around me whatsoever that the consumption of alcohol was an essential part of life.

My grandpa drank beer, he didn't drink alcohol. My grandma had sherry, not alcohol. Frank Domachowski drank alcohol.

At first I didn't know what alcohol was, really. My mother had rubbing alcohol and I didn't understand why people would drink that stuff. I didn't hook it up to manhattans, margaritas, and dancing on the beach with some hotties.

It was a sickness.

And there was a clear distinction from the time I was aware of the word.

There was the Alcoholics Anonymous and I understood what "anonymous" meant. It was quiet, it was private; we didn't tell anybody. Open and closed meetings? I understood that. We never talked, ever, out in public.

I got it. But it didn't make it a mystery. We just didn't talk about it; it wasn't talked about. It was so very, very simple. Clear.

To a young, impressionable consciousness, "That's that, and we don't speak of it." And there's a whole behavior when we're addressing it that we all do together in our privacy.

Because nobody in our neighborhood outside my family had anything to do with the alcoholic or the alcoholic behavior in any way, shape, or form that I'm aware of, that I ever saw.

We were the only ones that I knew, looking back. It's not like everyone was all, "Hey, how's your alcoholic doing in your bed basement?" "Oh, doin' pretty good, he's getting up there, about the fourth step now."

No! That didn't happen.

It was process; it was living process.

So my imprinting regarding alcohol as a substance didn't start to get loosened up in regards to my own consumption — until I was sixteen. And then there was an incident — when I was sixteen. My first incident…When I was sixteen — and prior to that, there was none, zero to my mouth.

The orientation — always, always, always — was alcohol and alcoholism is a sickness.

My parents' life was dedicated to being with other people who wanted to not have that sickness, who wanted to stop drinking and who wanted to have fun and be with each other and have another place to go and something else to do. Play cards, go bowling, go camping, go hunting, go fishing.

But first, there's the required turning it over and being with how bad it feels. And as quickly as possible would be best. Go through it.

But as a child, I watched people come up to and walk away and several women — some of the poorer, emotionally based women who were conflicted.

And a lot of it was natural.

Some of the women had intimate issues with, let's say, differently dysfunctional times and men. Hormones different, ages different, young women with older men — they had to drink it down. The natural urges needed to be drank down or replaced with some other behavior and that's kinda what happened. You could see that.

My mom had a lot of attractive women and single women because they were single women. There was no purpose in their lives. Something had occurred a while back and they had decided and found that alcohol worked.

And it does. It breaks the spell of one's own impairment.

It frees up attention so that a person can feel good for a while.

And then after another while, it doesn't feel so well and then a person wants to stop.

Or doesn't.

Well, those ladies were in hiccups and we'd go through periods and they were soft and gentle and spinsterly and alone and heartfelt.

I was at that age where I could be hugged and held, and I was hugged and held a lot. And that's how it was: I was available, just in the moment with anyone who was there in the moment of their vulnerability and I was innocently right there. And so I could be there for the breakthrough for them. Be there and watch them and let them know that it was all right. This is a passage and it hurts right now. Thank you so much for sharing that.

I didn't say that, but that's what you do as a listener in AA.

Those events, those spontaneous confessions, you never knew. Especially with the women who are drinking.

Now, I didn't follow my mother around on her tour of duty, but she usually had eight to ten women at a time — her babies. Until she moved back from California to Ohio; five to seven meetings per week, it was just ritual.

I have her fifty-year chip.

There's this atmosphere around the alcoholism that you think would just be the obvious deterrent for me personally, right?

No. "Why didn't I just know?"

The share — the stories — the places I'm gonna take you in my drinking — whew...take 'em slow; fast and furious; there were many.

A few close calls with the grim reaper. Got real lucky.

Those are the horror stories. Some people don't miss those curves. Some people miss the curve altogether and go off the road and die.

I didn't, but I did go off the road several times.

Those metaphors are terrible because inside of them are risks that are just irresponsible. And that's what we do — somehow in our wanting to dissolve into the absolute truth of life's enough if we are truly present.

Prior to that, drugs, sex, and rock 'n roll kick ass.

I've given you the set up now. We'll start to take a look at the next phase here, which is what happened at around my first night when I was sixteen with my friend Warren…And we decided to get drunk.

His mom was my mom's sponsee—wow, there's a story—anyway, he was my best friend and had been since he was seven and my mom had his back and his dad's back and everyone's back taking care of her and her drinking and drug use, which was really hard.

He and I were best friends and still are today. I just talked to him the day before yesterday. We cry because we're brothers and we didn't have the same parents. We didn't have brothers and sisters that loved us close to even half as much as we loved each other and love each other now. When I fell in 2001, I fell into his arms.

I started drinking—I had my first drink when I was seventeen with him.

I had my last drink right around him.

He was there to get me through that period of sobriety where I got the message and went out and started taking care of other guys, too.

Here we are.

The drunk-a-log gets thicker. . . . March, 1962.

SIX

1962 - My First Time Getting Drunk, & the Warning Unnoticed

In March of 1962, I was a senior at Grosse Point High School. Seventeen years old, finishing up my senior year, getting ready to go to Pennsylvania Military College the following fall.

Very excited about that.

It happened to be a unique window that I never saw open until the fact that it was open, and the condition was this:

My friend, Warren Kridler, who had been one of my best friends, and is my best friend now…His parents had taken off on a trip up north, my parents had gone on a trip up north with them, and my grandparents had gone to Florida and had left me with my grandmother's 1956 ..4-door Plymouth. My uncle Bud was a Chrysler Distributor up in Mount Pleasant, Bud Hubbell Motors, and he was very successful. Every year, everybody got a new car.

My grandmother just loved this Plymouth. It was a stick. She was 4'11", and she ran that 3-speed on the column, she was really good at driving. She also had left on this vacation, and decided that she was going to allow me to have her car for my senior year.

For me, having that opportunity gave me a lot of freedom — my parents are gone, and I picked up Warren, and he was going to spend the night. We had been dear friends, so we were always hanging out with each other.

Then we got this idea: Boy, let's try out drinking. The parents are gone; they won't be back until Tuesday. This is Friday, so we're good. So, if we go ahead and drink on Friday night after they leave, and we don't feel so — we'll have Saturday morning to recover. We can just kind of get — because we knew if we were going to get real drunk and we'd heard the stories, but we'd never had the experience.

We decided that we'd wait until his mom was gone, and then we'd go to his kitchen, and we looked up in the kitchen cabinet, and there was just—God, all sorts of different types of bottles, had no idea. But there were a couple of green bottles, and I just grabbed one and we put it in a bag—his gym bag—and we took it over to my house the day before the parents were gone.

Now, this is about 7:00 Friday night. We pull this bottle out, and we had some Verner's ginger ale, so we figured we'd mix it.

We were downstairs in my basement, and I had a Ping-Pong table down there—that was one of our favorite fun games to do—we had done it for years. When you'd get snowed in, you've got Ping-Pong, and that's about it—and another games, but that was fun.

It was a place where he and I had been comfortable down there, and so we decided to go ahead and we'd sit down and pour ourselves a glass of stuff, and kind of do half of the alcohol and then half of the ginger ale—that should be good.

We took this bottle and we split it. We had two really big glasses. We start taking a sip—aw, my God, it was just the worst tasting stuff, and we just—oh, God, it was so difficult—but we were having fun, starting to laugh.

We looked at the bottle. I said, do you know what this stuff is? He says, no.

We read it and it's like, V-E-R-M-O-U-T-H…Vermouth.

Okay, so we're drinking—we thought ver-mouth; we weren't sure what it was.

So, that's what it was VERMOUTH, and Verner's ginger ale.

It took us about five minutes to really kind of get it down. Within about 10-15-20 minutes, we kept asking each other, "How you feeling?" "I don't know, how are you feeling?" "How are you feeling?" "Are you feeling it yet?" "No, I'm not feeling it yet." And then, we just started talking, we couldn't—and there was a part of us, I believe, that really wanted to slur our words, so instead of being distinct...And we each had about 10 ounces of Vermouth in us.

Eventually, we were playing Ping-Pong, drunk and laughing—oh my God, just laughing hysterically, hysterically laughing, and stagger around, falling down. It was exactly what we thought, and it was just the most fun—he and I had the most fun, until—

There was the knock on the door.

Then there was a reality that started to creep in.

First of all, I had a pretty bad headache. Not feeling too good. The atmosphere in my mouth could not be—I had no idea what that was...And the pounding in my head...But then the pounding at the door...And I had found myself on the floor in my living room. There was somebody pounding on the door. I got up, and the sunshine and the door—I didn't know, I had no orientation to what was occurring, other than I knew I was very sick, and I felt like throwing up.

I saw a police officer standing at the door. I thought, oh my God. The police officer asked me, he says, "Is that your car across the street?" He steps back—it's my grandmother's Plymouth.

The rear end is just pretty much wiped out, the left rear just destroyed, the left rear panel pretty much gone. Glass all over the road.

I have no orientation at that moment of what's going on whatsoever. There's an unfamiliar buzzing; can't get oriented.

I tell the officer to please wait, and I go get my friend and wake him up, and we come out. I go outside and can barely see. I'm in my bare feet and it's cold. He said, "I want you to know that somebody drove by last night and hit that car."

I was relieved to know it wasn't me—that was my first response.

The next was, I'm not sure if he's right, because we didn't leave, so there wasn't anything that I could say that we got out in the car.

But, it was—my ride—it was gone. My life was changed. The headache was severe. Now what do I do?

My friend and I went back in the house and the next two, three, four, five hours were horrible—we had no clue how to dissuade the physiological experience that alcohol poisoning had created, and the disorientation to reality.

And of course, the two of us knew that, and I never touched alcohol again with the intention of drinking for—the fall of '63—boy, my life changed fast.

I was working in a factory, pregnant wife, bottle of beer—"Hey, it's the rookie!"

I was working at a factory—been married about three months—driving a hi-lo for the stamping plant at Chrysler out on Mound Road.

My first, second, and third beer were right there. I fell asleep getting in the toilet, and that was all that was. But then we moved to Lansing, and to East Lansing, and to Michigan State.

That's where my drinking started to have a habit. I started to have a pattern.

In 1964, I started my journey—it took '64 to 2004.

A long time, huh? Hold on.

SEVEN

1962 - My Honor Uncovered... A Silent Integrity Fights Back

1962. I had a moment where my life took over as my integrity faster than I could explain it or understand it in any kind of intellectual way.

All my life — my college thought life, definitely from tenth grade on, I wanted to go to West Point. There was no doubt about it. I had the avenue, because my brother was connected to the senator. They were roommates at Michigan. I wasn't a good student, but everybody knew me and my family, and I was able to know myself there. Even though I wasn't able to excel at sports in high school, something happened during my time there, and I had to take growth hormones and thyroid. I didn't really start growing until I was actually hitting 18.

But in this situation, I'd always wanted to attend West Point. During that time, they had every program on TV — West Point at 10:00, and Annapolis at 10:30, and Corp Cadets. I wanted that more than anything. I'd been raised an only child. I had some good friends.

But there was something deep, deep in me. I knew my grandfather died in the war. I knew how my father spoke about him. Both my brothers had been in WWII and the Korean War.

I wasn't really able to fulfill being on a football team, because my growth happened off schedule. I wasn't hitting my prime when I was 16. It really didn't happen until later in my 20s actually, for me.

But this situation in September and October of 1962 was I'd been allowed to matriculate through Pennsylvania Military College, and I was very pumped up. You got the uniform, the hazing, the bracing.

I'd been working out for a year getting ready.

My dad said he'd pay for it. I wanted it more than anything.

I had great anticipation of the brotherhood there...Maybe we'd die together or something.

I'd kind of had a fascination with dying for a cause as a kid — I don't know why. I used to keep a cartoon book — it was just like one or two pages long — about this kid who stood in the middle of two families, and cut down a tree and died. But the families were brought together.

It's silly stuff that kids feel is worthwhile, to give up their life for.

But when I got to military college, it didn't feel that way, for me, when we got down to a certain moment.

I was ready for everything else — locker was clean, I was integrating well.

Sir, the cow's fine: She walks, she talks, she's full of chalk...the lacteal fluid extracted from the female of the bovine species is highly prolific to the Nth degree...

...mutherucker !

You never know where you'll find betrayal. But I know what it looks like. And I found it there...Where I thought I'd find a brotherhood.

I ran smack up against reality of someone else's mean dominance of my innocence.

I'm coming out of my room, and he looks at the picture of Mary Kay on my desk and says, "Who's the whore? "

I mean, before I turned, I knew I was going to break his nose.

My life changed there and I hated that moment. Behind my back, said something like that to me.

You go to the captain, and then to the brigade commander. He says, "Well, Hubbell, here's the good thing: Your classmates want you as president."

It was over—president of what, a bunch of maniacs?

Anyway, see these things about yourself. Who do you tell? Who cares? Who listens, right?

I'd do it again in a heartbeat.

It's that edge. It's just not a fucking thought; give it up. The tone—we have to be gentle with each other.

We don't want to push people into their survival, such that they lash out physically.

But I didn't know that I lived in a culture of men that would attack another guy at his heart when he was already standing in his honor for him.

It gets you really pissed. There you go.

EIGHT

1963 - Life's Commitments Takeover

After getting home from military college — which didn't work out…I didn't find what I wanted there because I wanted a culture of young men who shared the vision I had of serving our country and dying together. And I found that there were young men whose behavior were being modified by being residents of this pre-West Point military college. More by correction than by choice.

I ended up having a fight with an individual of that illness and abuse, and they kicked me out. Another time where my intuition made a decision for me and in the face of two years' preparation, I left.

So now — fall 1962. I'm a benign 18-year-old — not much going on, except I'm in love with my girlfriend, Mary Kay, and she's a sweetheart. Beautiful girl. Innocent. Loving.

We made that connection that summer — first love — and the natural chemistry was starting to take over. Both of us were very, very ready and both of us were…new. That relatedness was gentle and sweet and soft, and just like it should have been for first love.

During that fall I enrolled at Wayne State University and became a full time student for the winter and spring terms..

During and Christmas, in through the winter months, she and I went through a little check, check, double-check — do we really want to be committed? She was still just finishing up tenth grade.

Mary Kay was a student at Cass Technical High School in downtown Detroit. She happened to be one of those gifted musicians and dedicated cellists that was seen when she was young; and she was invited by the Detroit Women's Symphony Orchestra to participate as a member of their symphony at fifteen.

We were uncomplicated together. She'd go down to Cass Tech every morning, take the bus down there, and her and Diana Ross and some of the other Motown folks that were just high school kids, 1960-63.

She was a gentle soul, and our relationship became deep and committed and firm, and was a foundation for me going into military school.

I looked forward to that, and I looked forward to and held onto the image of our relationship.

But as we moved into the spring and summer, organic nature took its course, and off I went to be a counselor on a camp up near Travers City, and I got the phone call that she was pregnant.

My life changed.

In July of 1963, a 17-year old and 18-year old, Mary Kay Wallace and Bruce David Hubbell, got married.

We didn't know…We started to live with her folks, and that wasn't very comfortable.

It was a time of very tense doubt.

I didn't know quite what to do.

My life had been completely disrupted from the destiny that I thought I was going to have — just going on with Wayne State and continue on, and I thought engineering. I was going to go to General Motors, because I was good at engineering. I was good in math and science.

But the reality of a pregnant wife and the need for work put me out there immediately. My grandfather challenged me to be responsible — get a job.

My mother wanted the easy way out, which was to have an abortion, and that conversation lasted 10 seconds when I told her, don't you ever say that to me again — loudly, three times. She understood, that was it. She didn't like the answer, but that was what was going to be — Mary Kay and I were getting married.

So, that moment of taking over my life and taking over responsibility for all the choices I was making started to take hold. There was that deeper sense of becoming a young man, as opposed to being an adolescent like I was at 18, to continue to dig the rock n' roll.

But at the same time, I didn't realize that there was a shield being thrown around my life.

Vietnam was coming, and I was ripe bait.

Even though I was married, I still got called up. We'll pick up that later when we hit about 1967-68.

So now, I'm in a place of being married and looking for work.

We've got the big car companies. I went around to every one of them, and I loved General Motors, but I couldn't get in there.

So I heard about a job at the Chrysler factory over on Mound Road Stamping Plant. That became an immediate source of income.

But, there was a disconnect between my wife and myself. What should have been the sanctuary of a young couple's love nest — we were in her brother's bedroom at her parents' house on a set of springs you couldn't even — box springs uncovered. Our urges were at best now relished to the floor. It was horrible.

You couldn't be who you were as an adolescent and…in respect to my abilities, I just had to go do it.

At $1.35/hour, I went to work for Chrysler Corporation at the Mound Stamping Plant. I worked there during the Kennedy assassination, and that whole horrible event, and that was just about the time…It was the time when I had my second experience with drinking.

It was an evening job. I was a hi-low driver for the Chrysler

Stamping Plant.

What my job was…As fenders came off the production line, quarter panels…hoods…tops…doors…We put them in racks, because each piece got stamped out initially, and then it was take on in its stamping process. But when you were at the big stampers, they were just stamping out the doors from the sheet metal, they would stack them and 5, 10, 15 standing tall on these wooden pallets, and then I would pick the pallet up with the hi-low, and take it back and put it into the inventory. Then I'd take the empty pallets, these racks — because they're different shapes and sizes depending on what came off — you couldn't put a hood on top of a fender one, so each one had a different — you had to keep the lines going, so we had to have a rack there, so they could put the hoods on, and then we had to take the racks off that were finished, over and put them away. So we were constantly moving.

There are some lines, when you got assigned as a hi-low driver, you get some lines that are slow as hell. And that was kind of cool, because then you'd be able to kick it.

I worked my tail off to become a hi-low driver. I started off in the lines, and it was like two months later, myself and another kid and I — we were Detroit boys, exceptional drivers who really knew how to handle wheels — we could flip those hi-lows in circles, it was all fun. They were just tinker toys for us. And we had a blast.

We also had some hi-low drivers, of course, who were the veterans — they had been there for ten years driving hi-low. This guy, Neil Steel, dropped dead of a heart attack one day. But he looked like Rock Hudson — he was gorgeous, dainty, sweet, fun.

He and a couple other guys we'd used to call Peanuts and Moonlight — everyone had a nickname; I was "the kid" — Steel came up and he was like, "Hey, kid, why don't you come have lunch with us?" Lunch was dinner, and dinner…I went to school in the mornings. I didn't get home from the factory until like 1:15, but I was up and out of there by 7:15, so I'd get five hours of sleep, but that was okay.

In that fall I was off to Wayne State and I was there for about five weeks; but then I dumped Wayne State, I just said, "I can't; I need to stay at work."

For the first five weeks, I was working there, burning the candle at both ends. I was on the afternoon shift. We clocked in around 3:30 and punched out at midnight, so we had our eight and a half. And a half hour lunch, which we kind of had to pay for because of the extra half hour you didn't get paid for…Two fifteen minute breaks, depending on what the jobs were. Some of them got breaks because they were on production. Some of the door inserts guys

I cut my wrist badly. Bleeding everywhere…I was going too fast and sliced my wrist open. I was on one of the stamping plant lines that did the parts and pieces on the inside. All of us coordinated together — this was a stamping plant, we just stamped out all the parts and pieces for the construction of the body and prepared the pieces for assembly.

Steel invites me, and Peanut…They want to take me out for "lunch" — which was at eight, it was dark — I remember distinctly, it was just — I was a kid — they liked me, it was fun, and we enjoyed each other. …"Grosse Pointe, your dad's an attorney, yeah, he he he, I've heard about you." There was always fun, laughter, enjoyment.

This one night, Steel said, "Listen, we got some beer. We wanna take you out and get you drunk."

I thought…"Fuck, okay, why not?"

So I got initiated with the guys. Three beers in a half hour break. They extended it another half our, kind of overlapped it…We okayed it with the supervisor. He was kind of in on it. We were way ahead on work; so we were way good as a team. This was kind of a boys' night out.

They kind of baptized me that night.

We were coming back — at 9:30, I was done. They were laughing. I went into the toilet and fell asleep with my pants down. Just on my face. They just thought that was hysterical.

The second baptism was, "No, thank you very much."

And that was it.

Now we move into the time where I get ready to make a transition.

NINE

1964 - Opportunity Calls — MSU — The Cost of Hidden FUN — 40 Years' Worth

In January of 1964, Mary Kay was getting ready to have Robin.

I'm still working at the factory, and I had a really good buddy of mine in high school who'd been accepted to Michigan State. I hadn't, because my grades were too low, and that's why my dad was able to buy my first year at the military school, with the intention of having my grades go up, and take some time going through the courses.

I was intended to be at PMC two years and then go to West Point. I was willing to do six to get my First Lieutenant. I knew that was okay with me. I didn't care, I was 18 — what, 24, I didn't care.

So that was the plan. But here we are.

Rick Yeomans, my good buddy in high school, called me up and said, "Bruce, you should apply to Michigan State."

I said, "Rick, I already did, and they turned me down."

He says, "I know that, but you went to Wayne State, you've got a couple of quarters in at Wayne, and why don't you reapply to Michigan State? I just talked to one of the counselors and they said that if you took the entrance exam and you score above 75%, they have to let you in. It's just as cheap to live up there as it is for you to live down here, and you can live in married housing."

I was like, "What, wow, Rick, really?"

He says, "Yeah, come on up. Here's the counselor's name."

It didn't take me long to go up there, take the test. I was called and told that I had scored in the 95th percentile of entering freshmen.

With my background at Grosse Pointe High School, even though I had Cs, and my SATs were very weird, because I had a 720 math, and a 280 English, because I could not read, it just wasn't there.

What I have come to see is I didn't have the ability for comprehension because if you gave me a word I didn't understand, I couldn't go on. It was like a hiccup. I couldn't get beyond words I didn't understand and continue to think I knew what I was reading.

I didn't have enough interest in the material anyway, so I didn't bother.

The verbal didn't get pulled out so much in the testing, I guess, as a dysfunction. I flew by with colors, they say.

I talked to my father, and it was a deal — it was $105 a month for married housing, including a phone and electricity. It was a one-bedroom — actually, we got a two-bedroom for $105; it was $95 for a one-bedroom. But we wanted a bedroom for Robin and one for ourselves.

That was great. I started spring term of '64, and I was into it.

I immediately jumped in, decided to go into where I left off, which was engineering. But I was more interested in physics as a science. I just loved the idea of the potential at what physics was talking about.

One of the privileges I had growing up was a young man in my life, Ken Davis. Ken ended up getting his PhD. ...a real nuclear physicist, a "rocket scientist."

When Ken and I met at 12 years old, I didn't know anything about Einstein. Within 45 days of meeting him, I understood the Special Theory of Relativity — that interested me: the fact that I could get that, that I could get the ball bouncing here, as opposed to a boy bouncing a ball on a train going past me. I could see the zigzag of the movement of the ball in virtual space, as Kenny pointed it out.

He had a book about the Special Theory of Relativity, and we studied it together. He just pointed out the simplicity of that idea. It was a kind of theoretical physics that I was very drawn to.

When I got to Michigan State and went into the school of Mathematics. I was just doing the basics. I didn't have to declare a major, but I wanted to. I was starting to take physics right off.

The first day I walked into the hall of the physics department, it was the most…It was like walking into — it just felt — the more I walked in, the darker it got.

It was literally a physical event for me. It wasn't like I was walking into a building; it's like I was walking into these deep, dark halls, and it felt like that; it looked like that. It felt like someone had turned the lights out, literally. I couldn't even go see the counselor.

I went to the admissions and just decided I'm not going to declare anything. I was just going to stay with my experience of looking for a major. But I didn't want to do physics.

I found out by fall of 1964 that I wanted to do veterinary medicine. I found that out in the summer. I applied and was accepted to the pre-vet school. I'd had my destiny there set forth for the next 12 to 14 months.

Now in moving up to Michigan State and the primal event of just making a decision now that I had to choose a life…I had to choose a career. It was like throwing darts in the dark, because you knew what a dart felt like, but you had no idea what you were throwing at. I had no idea about anything that there was a career, or what a career felt like.

I was 18 years old. Just turning 19.

I didn't have the capacity — other than to go to work, pay the bills, get the money from my dad, help Mary Kay with the baby, take care of her, have time with her, spend time with her.

We were doing all right.

But as far as thinking outside the box, as far as the expansion outside of the experience of surviving day to day, and career, and what are you going to do—I was all impulse, all impulse. It's the impulse of what I had. There wasn't anything in my impulses; my impulsive behavior was not dysfunctional. It was impulsive, it was adolescent; it's what we're supposed to do.

If our parents imprint us correctly, which my parents did, which we know—I was there as a 19-year old guy, married with a daughter now at Michigan State—but there was something else coming. It was the natural part of being a man that was coming, and it was coming in the form of a phone call.

It was from a friend of mine, Tommy Brown.

Tommy had been one of the most popular guys at Grosse Pointe High School.

He called me up from University of Michigan and said, "Hey, Bruce, I'm in a fraternity here. Why don't you come on down and come to a fraternity party?"

I looked at my wife, and I said, "What do you mean?

He said, "Yeah, why don't you come on down Friday, we have a — we drink on Fridays."

That was the moment.

I decided, either I go down and see Tom and drink and lie about it and then come back...or I don't go.

Obviously, I didn't alert my wife that I'd saw that choice in front of me.

I told Tommy, "Yeah."

Then I asked her, "Mary Kay," —after I hung up—"my friend Tom is down at University of Michigan. Would you mind if I went down there and he's got a fraternity, and I'm going to go spend the night with him down there. Do you mind?"

No, I didn't say anything about the partying or the drinking.

I was so excited; I couldn't wait to get down there. I was panicked. There was this sense of adventure, this sense of freedom, this sense that it was the tip of something.

It was the tip that I had freedom, and the freedom that I chose for my life there was the freedom based on hiding, and not being honest—kind of like being covertly hostile—passive/aggressive.

Now, why wouldn't I be able to read passive/aggressive? Isn't this fucking interesting?

Okay, I'm serious. Here we are, drunk-a-log Chapter seven or something.

It was that first moment, right there with Tommy Brown and the phone call and the first conscious drink.

That is when I decided to be passive/aggressive.

I introduced it in my life, so I had to support the shit.

I had to support others in lying; I did forever.

I lied and I betrayed my wife forever, from that place of—because I'd made a decision to lie, and I forgot that that one lie started it all—that I was unaccountable to myself.

I lied.

Where in my wholeness do I say, lying is appropriate, especially when the intention is to deceive?

There's a difference to not tell someone, or to actually misguide someone, or to purposefully, for the safety of yourself or another deceive; but not in the adolescent survival of wanting to manipulate another's heart — which hers was open and simple — as a just coming on 18-year-old girl.

<u>There it was. There it is now.</u>

There it is, my life going right by, just like that car going right by.

Somewhere in April of 1964, I decided I'd lie and forget about it.

I get a chance to **make amends to myself for that.**

I've handled everybody else.

Man, if you haven't done a drunk-a-log, jump on it.

TEN

2001 - 37 Years to Take My First Step
In five minutes I Committed to be a Sponsor

April 30, 2001: I'm getting ready to make a phone call to a friend of mine, Warren — for I'm ready to take the 1st step.

In the next 72 hours, my life will be turned over. It'll happen in 40 seconds.

It's the first 40 seconds when I met my sponsor, Jimmy Gent.

He didn't ask me if I wanted to be his sponsee, or sponsorees, as they call it in Oklahoma.

No, he didn't ask me that.

What he asked me was, what are you doing tomorrow night? I said, I don't know. He said, well, I'll tell you what, you be at my house, 6:00, and we're going to go to 1st step. It's the men's recovery center outside of Oklahoma City. It's where the boys from the DOC go when they have that last chance to take responsibility or go to prison. There's no jail for these boys. They're looking at hard time or cleaning up their act. So nobody's fooling around out there, 1st step; everybody's on purpose, on target, and they want to recover.

And it's a very, very intense scene for me.

Sunday afternoon at 6:00, Jimmy Gent's home, I show up. Jimmy was pretty clear with me. He wasn't going to fool around at all.

He was wondering; he said, "Look, I'm going to be real straight with you, it's usually 1, 2, three and you're out. "...he wasn't talking about strikes...he's talking about the steps.

He was talking about sincerity that people have in recovery; but when it comes to action, it always starts with a question; it's always just the first question.

But you can't ask that question—you can't ask the first question until the person is ready to answer.

Now, good sponsors, skilled sponsors, serious sponsors know that this is a life-or-death situation for anyone who wants to get sober, truly. What we have is a moment; we have a moment to look, but we can't look ourselves, we have to be asked to look, and we have to be ready to look.

Jimmy G. sponsored 20 men at a time.

At 6:00pm May6, 2001: he said, here's a yellow pad. Are you ready, Bruce?

And I was ready. I said, yeah, yes.

He looked at me and said, I'm going to ask you three questions right now:

Are you powerless over alcohol; is your life unmanageable? I said, yes.

He says: Do you believe that a power greater than you will restore you to sanity? I said, yes.

He said: Are you ready to make a decision to turn your will on your life over to the care of God as you understand Him? I said, yeah.

He says: We're done with the first three steps.

Now, I want you to take that pad, and over the next two months, I want you to start working the 4th step. I want you to write down every name of every person you ever can think of; in the left column, I want you to leave a space—

I don't want you to do anything, but I want you to write their names.

I want you to leave a lot of space between your parents and your brothers and sisters, wives and relatives. In the space moving to the right in those columns, I want you to write down just a note of what fear, resentment, anger that you have in your thoughts that has anything to do with any of those people—write it down. Then I want you to write how you felt about that experience—write it down.

When you're ready, I want you to let me know that you're ready, and I'll check in with you.

Now, the other thing I want you to do is that when we get the 1st step tonight, I want you to find three men to sponsor. I want you to take care of them. I want you to not be selfish.

The only way you're going to get this is if you start taking care of other people.

 Do you understand? I said, yes.

It took me 37 years to be ready to take the First Step authentically as an alcoholic!

It took me about 40 seconds to prepare myself for the 4th step.

That and right there; at Jimmy G's home...THAT became the true journey of my recovery.

It's from that day in 2001, where I was asked if I were powerless—and I was, and I was ready, and I took that First Step.

ELEVEN

2001 - I Turn it OVER

2001 is a long time away — 1964. I have no idea the 37 years, of course that lay ahead of me as a 20-year old man with responsibilities to take care of his own personal business.

2001 there wasn't anything left — it's just me, a car, and my stuff.

Those 37 years had a lot of time, had a lot of moments of choosing to reach for a drink with no sense of the "ism" of the alcohol, just a certainty that it was going to work, it was going to relieve me and distract me and give me the freedom I wanted from whatever I was dealing, and dealing with poorly.

But those 37 years are not years on the streets of San Francisco in the gutter; though I did that one night just to remind myself when I was at my bottom that I was on the bottom, on the street in San Francisco — I did that in 1997 — on the bottom, on the streets of San Francisco, laying there. I wanted to feel it, I wanted to be a real alcoholic.

I wanted to be laying on the street drunk watching the people's feet, listening to the noise the cable cars and the dead motionless impact of unused life. It was exactly what I thought it was — it was empty, it was soulless, and there wasn't anything left.

After sleeping for a while, I got up — I'd had enough,.... but I hadn't stopped drinking yet.

So these 37 years from 1964 to 2001, they weren't all drunk — no way.

And the times of drinking weren't all bad — no way.

It was fun, a lot of camaraderie, a lot of times of just smiles and giggles — and a lot of lying, a whole lot of lying.

Nobody ever talked about that; nobody ever talked about the fact that we lie to manipulate, that we lie to deceive; that we lie to take people's trust away, and then blame them and shame them for not supporting us, and finding a bunch of other folks who we don't know to agree with us in some hole somewhere.

So those 37 years of fear, sorrow, anger, boredom, doubt, discomfort, and irritable, restless and discontent — the stories are there. Even though I knew, I took that first step. There was a whole lot of steps that were taken in the wrong direction.

So that's where we're headed now — we're going to go back to 1964.

We're going to look into the soul and the heart of that young man, and we're going to talk about his surroundings, we're going to talk about his circumstance, we'll talk about his heart and reveal his intentions, and we'll see how his lies changed his life until the day he gave it over 37 years later; even then, the tough part was just beginning.

So now the stage is set. Most of the major players are in place. We see that there's going to be a 37-year run here, before the final curtain comes down on the ignorance and the avoidance and the irresponsibility to stand up in the midst of death and the certainty of it, the confound confront — it isn't going away.

There's a whole lot of life maybe there, maybe.

And is it really just one step at a time?

Or is it are those that make this instantaneous miracle quantum leap, and then the bills are paid?

It all slips by me so fast in the moment of — do I want to stop, do I want to interrupt?

What is the thread really; is it taking us anywhere, is it taking me anywhere? Why does it feel so hauntingly attractive?

Why do I see it out of the corner of my eye and my heart leaps for its presence—what is it? It seems to change; it seems to shimmer; it seems to sing and to call into flavors and intersections of dance, the touch and the play and the deep, deep free abandonment, lost in the joy, lost in the laughter, free in the ecstasy beyond measure, knowing one is tethered somewhere.

But for a moment, I'm free—I'm free and I float, and I allow this wonderful partner to show up in the eyes and the sounds and the tastes; but it isn't in the objects, it's a deeper creating, it's a dance of the soul of my yearning to be on fire, gone in my heart of the thrill of the moment of my own trust.

That even in the presence of smells and sounds, the thread is still there...and so, it can't be in the sounds, and it can't be in the smells, and it can't be in the taste—it can't be. but I can't turn away—not now, not as a 20-year old man—no...I must know, I must travel that road, I must—and I'm going to it now.

It's over, I made the choice, and I look forward to the dance, and I look forward to the invitation.

So I stay open, and I stay open.

TWELVE

1964 - The Journey to my Freedom & Sanity Begins
on the Road Less Traveled

We see in the space of that young man there—like in all young men—it's easy to sing the song if you stand and have stood there. It was easy to listen to, too.

That's what this is about—it's not about the story, it's about the listening.

It's okay now, it's really okay now…

So the gentle story continues.

The relationship with Mary Kay was sweet and gentle. Days on campus are exciting—the classes, the size, the immensity of the campus, the thrill of other people my age and the youth and the enthusiasm gave a tenor to the space of this undisturbed moment of human maturity going through its adolescence.

I don't mean to be abstract about that. But it was very clear, that if you were a student at Michigan State, you were given a little bit of license—you're supposed to kick it up, you're supposed to get it on, you're supposed to get fucked up and do what you do. This is the time, but this is the time, not more.

So it's the time to get in to try it on, the social dance of the deal with alcohol was very open.

If you're drinking too much, a cop would just tell you, "Hey, just go home."

Alcohol was not considered an issue, nor was anybody monitoring the 18-19 year olds, and the 21-year old drinking age.

The culture itself, there in the early part of the '60s, was starting to change. The music was starting to go and come out into the bars, the bars starting to open up and have bands.

In '64, the Beatles, of course, were raging, and then in '65, coming on strong.

And you've got this distinction of life free in the college level; and yet, for myself, I still had the responsibility to work and bring in money and to go to school.

But the pulse of the times and the call of my friends was too enchanting, and took me over. I looked forward to them inviting me, and I kept hoping after this time with Tom that something would occur, and there did.

I caused this one, and the rest of them were these runs.

They would start before it even started and Mary Kay never saw it coming.

It was just time with me and my buddies — I need time away, she'd go be with her mom.

But the truth was that she was receiving less and less of my authentic attention, for even in the midst of the school and the hitting the dots and all of that, I was…The only thing I wanted to do was party. I couldn't wait to get down to Albion, or go back to Michigan.

So the spring and summer of '64 were starting to be the calls outside of the commitment, and there are the calls based on the door that alcohol opened up and I knew would open up — the incredible adventure of the playfulness.

Warren, a friend of mine, invited me down once, and there was dancing. To make a long story short, I got hooked up with a girl, and I lied because it was easier now. But I took the ring off, but it was easier now.

And it was always easier after that event, because I could just turn it off and turn it on.

Maybe she did know.

That one day, she came up and said—saying she talked to her mom about a divorce; she was saying, "I've known all along…So, yeah, I'm way ahead of you here in your game…"

That was to be played out, and that was five years away.

Interwoven through there is this connected energy of looking and participating the authenticity of what's attractive, what's real and authentic, even if it appears to go to dance on the dark side, which that's all it was, was the dancing—it wasn't like heroin and crack cocaine—it wasn't that; but it was the hiding, it was the lying, and it was like two lives…

I mean, wife and two kids. Eventually, you know, I got the fact that I couldn't have the two lives, which was the alcoholic life away.

But it started to begin there—the adventure started to begin there, and I could tolerate the lying, because of the payoff of the thrill. And then it gets mixed, it got mixed, but I didn't care—the "I don't care" got put up as some way of guaranteeing that I didn't have to look. But I didn't care was an action, it was a turning away from, it was an avoidance.

What else, what else?

If I'm not looking at her and I'm looking away, she doesn't exist. I'm looking in front and say, "Ooh, what do I want to choose today," without her being there.

Why? Because I just turned my back. Does she know? No. I did it in my head—yes. Am I here with her in the conversation? No. Where am I? I'm looking away.

I'm looking away to the phone call, for the call from my friend to the date and the time and the event of the chaotic ecstasy. I can see it now.

What was it that you said, Mary Kay?

That area, that skill set was starting to develop itself, it was working — the payoff was being delivered, the power was being secured.

I can write my own ticket. All's I have to do is lie.

THIRTEEN

PERSONAL Side Note — For Honesty and Thoroughness

In order for this to be completely thorough, I'm going to need to say some extremely personal things — some of which, if this does go to print, will probably be removed because of the exposure of other peoples' lives and the things I'm going to say about them, especially my intimacy with my wife.

There're conditions around that intimacy that preclude me — in fact, I'll just go ahead and say this now, so that we have a general understanding of my relationship to sexuality:

My mother was the most beautiful female of beautiful females in the classic sense, in all senses. When she was plain, she was, to me, the most beautifully kind of dressed plainness; and when she dressed up, and she turned on the diva, I felt embarrassed, because the sexual female was in full bloom. My dad loved it.

She was a true diva, she was a true fully-incarnated female. She knew, after coming through the '30s and the '40s, that men and women loved attractive women. My mother was an attractive woman.

She dressed, and when they wanted to be playful, you know, she wore the tight sweaters, she wore the red lipstick, she wore the tight pants. She played with men in front of my father, and that was fine.

There was a dominance in her that she had taken responsibility for herself — that I am, yes, very beautiful, and yes, I'm very attractive, and aren't you lucky to be playing with me right now.

She was always playful like that.

She understood the gift of her beauty, and she understood that she also had a swagger about her adult point of view of what was real and what was false.

So that, for me, in my intimate relationship with Mary Kay, was very powerful. It took right off the very first night we met. It was just instantaneous. We were deeply involved in the total organic event of falling in love, and the sensuality of it all.

But it took us many, many months before we started to be able to have relations, and they were difficult and clunky, and here and there.

Then as the year moved on in '63, our intimacy became a daily event; and it seemed on the weekends, we'd go to movies and drive-ins and bring changes of clothes, so that when she would go home, she looked okay for her mom. We were definitely in the throes of the passion of young love — there wasn't any doubt about it, and we were into it.

But then there came a time in that young love when the passion of the female overtook that capacity of the male, and I started to pull back on my natural desire, for hers seemed to be unquenchable, and I'd run out of gas.

And that started to concern me, and give me an insecurity in regards to my own sexuality. That has remained with me the majority of our life, and caused me to avoid certain types of situations with women, and never got involved in any kind of prurient or weird sexual encounters.

In my free days ahead, which are to come here, there were many occasions that I had to be close to other women — but the dysfunction and the disconnect and the sense of not being able to tell the truth really set a course in my intimacy for my sexuality with my wife.

So that by the time we got to that moment, 1969, where she informed me that she had talked to her mom about a divorce, she had found a lover in my friend — it makes sense now.

I can see it, and the disconnect had started years before — the real connect, the deep I-trust-you connect, I-can-trust-you-loving-me connect, and our intimacy-as-an-expression-of-my-joy-of-the-ecstasy-I'm-feeling-with-you connect.

So those types of bondings that would have/could have/should have kept me secure in my deep intimacy with my beautiful wife and loving friend…But it wasn't happening. So the background about my cautions, the background about my orientations, the background of my yearnings and needs, never really took on anything in the sexual area.

It was a deeper yearning.

It was something that I wanted that I couldn't find, and I wasn't going to find it until after I had gone through recovery, and I was able to stand in my own experience being whole and complete.

That wasn't to happen for over 40 years.

FOURTEEN

1965 - The Space of No Space

I had a clear moment of emancipation with my father. It was almost violent, and it took about a month to run its course.

In 1965, in August, I had a moment where outside of any thinking, I realized that I no longer could trust my father, for he didn't know me, and I couldn't tell him that he didn't know me, for in the moment, the way he was speaking to me pre-empted my ability to know anything, for I was an asshole, I was ignorant, I was stupid, and I was throwing my life away, and I was an idiot.

I received that news in the presence of my wife, who is 19 and just had our second child. I had made a decision that changed my father's opinion of me, and I knew that.

In 1964, I had developed — because I applied for the veterinary school — I found that I had a gift in animal husbandry, and I was trained and taught how to examine, judge and rate livestock by Dr. Harlan Ritchie, Professor of Animal Husbandry and Gary Minish Ph.D. at Michigan State University.

I demonstrated this gift by being first out of 466 students, including all of the FFA kids in An Hub, Animal Husbandry 101, and the top 15 went to the livestock judging team, to which I was on in the winter and spring of '65 at Michigan State. I liked it, I enjoyed it. Also, I took a job, while I was taking full-time credits, working for a veterinary firm, because I wanted to get the feel for veterinary medicine — we needed some extra income, and I have extra hours. I mean, school — you just had to kind of show up for class — not always. So you didn't have to be there all the time; you just had to make sure you hit the subjects. It wasn't that difficult; you could actually go to school and work if you were smart enough — and I was, so I could handle stuff like that.

We were living in married housing, and had been cramped. A friend of mine had been driving a truck for a cleaning company. I took a job there in the summer, even after getting accepted to vet school. In the fall, I was going to start in vet school. I'd been given a grant, I was liked. I was going to be on the livestock judging team at Michigan State, and that gave me some bennies.

But for me, something wasn't right. I didn't like the doctors, the vets that I worked for. They liked taking advantage of people; they liked seeing how much money they could make, how much they could charge. It was like a game, like every day pulling the slot machine — we did $450 today — kind of like high flying on cash register, and irrespective of what happened with the animals. I didn't like that.

Also, on the Michigan State side where the livestock judgment team was, I was understanding that there was a great covert derision toward me — a city boy who just could see animals, and could talk about them better than the kids that had been in the programs and grew up on farms. I didn't realize that I was not well liked, but I found out by the middle of spring quarter. I didn't want to be on the team anymore, and I couldn't deal with that choice.

So, my friend got me this job with a trucking company just driving a truck. The owner of the company said, "Listen, I'm going to pay you $20,000 a year, come work for me" — and my jaw dropped. That was unheard of money. Said, "I want you to come sell for me."

We'd moved out onto a farm. I was happy — are you kidding?

Now, he gave me conditions and all of that, but I could make that by selling, and I could see that I could do it and I liked it. It was fun, it was interesting, and I liked him and his dad — Chacola Cleaning Materials.

So I decided, I don't want to do the thing with Michigan State with the — you know, it was fine that I was good at An Hub, but I didn't like where I was going. I certainly didn't like the people.

I was afraid of them, I didn't understand why they treated me the way the treated me. I kind of did a little, but I didn't want to deal with it. I had so much other — I got a wife and two kids. I'm working, and then the thing with the vets…I just blew it out of the water. I didn't want to be standing in a white coat with a lot of smelly chemicals, waiting to sell dog food.

I made an executive decision when I talked to Mary Kay and I said, hey — we moved into this farm, it was fabulous, big ass farm — we loved it, loved it. I'd spent a couple of months working at this company, and it was happening.

So I went to see my dad and my mom, and I told Mary Kay, boy, we gotta go talk to my parents, because my dad's been funding me, along with the other money. You know, I'd started to work — tried to pull the factory thing off and go to school, but that didn't work, that just burned me out. Tried to work in the car factory and go to school — not "or." So as a situation, I had talked to my mom and dad about this. Mary Kay and I went up there — our house in Grosse Pointe — and said, "Mom and dad, we've got to talk to you." My dad wasn't sure what was coming. I mean, I was always getting a little bit outside of his comfort area, even though he had had to get married, you know. I was hitting the dots. You know, I'd had a couple of hiccups, but nothing dramatic.

Mary Kay and I walked in and we've got Robin and she's barely 2 — not even 2 — we got Amy in the basket.

I tell them, "I'm not going back to school, and I'm not going to be on the livestock judging team, I'm not going to vet school. I'm going to work for this cleaning company selling cleaning supplies. Mary Kay and I are going to live in Holt, on a farm, and we may have an opportunity to buy it. I think I'd like to raise cattle and do some farming, but I want to do this cleaning job."

My dad went retro, and yelled at me and shamed me.

He became so angry that the part in me that was triggered as a child, again, just took over, and there became as if he was talking and I was just starting to look around the room, because he was off and he was lecturing me, like he did, which I don't remember much.

But he wasn't going to be done, he was going to say things to me, and then a calmness came about me. It felt like it happened in an instant, but it felt like it took a long time.

I thought, huh, okay, okay, now let's see, I've got about $3,000 in the bank. I've got my passbook in my mother's bottom drawer. I can excuse myself after he's done, and I can go in there and get that—nobody's going to know that—I'll put that in my back pocket. I'll go to the bathroom, flush the toilet, come back and sit down. And then, I'll excuse Mary Kay and I, tell my dad I think he's right, but then I'm going to get in the car, and I'm going to take Mary Kay, and I'm going to take her home—close to home. On the way, I'm going to cash…Go to the bank and take out the $3,000. I'm going to have her drop me off and tell her that I don't know who I am anymore.

And that's exactly what I did.

In a matter of an hour-and-a-half later, I was standing on a street in Detroit, and my wife and my two kids were driving away in our Valiant, and I was standing there with $3,000 in my pocket. I had no clue where I was going to go. But the last thing I said to my wife was—I looked at her and said, "I don't know who I am anymore. I can't come back until I do. I'm sorry."

She knew that I was—she saw it go down. She says, "What do you want me to do?" You know, we were right at the corner. I said, "You go to your mother's now," and I gave her $1,000 and said, "You take care, okay? I'm sorry to leave you like this."

She didn't see me again for another six weeks. That was a game changer.

My father never, never, never ever crossed me, interfered me, corrected me—or as he said, and apologized for—I took your inventory, son, and that was a mistake of mine, and I'll never do it again.

He kept his word.

FIFTEEN

1965 - Deeper Found Intimacy

So, on the street corner there in 1965 — I can remember the corner, I can see the Valiant as it drives away. But before we move on to what happens over the next six weeks, we've now uncovered more of a formal thinking matrix of behavior. Unknown to myself, I have chosen to be alone, not in a way that I understood as something that I responsibly said — I'm here as one person, I'm here, I'm ready — it wasn't anything like that. I had chosen the back door of lying because it worked. I was clear I could always get out of any situations — I just needed to manipulate others' attention, and then get out. As the years have gone on, I have become better at that — except for those who lie better than me, and there were many over those 35 to 40 years.

That young man that was standing there on the corner in 1965, a couple of grand in his pocket — life stopped. There's no past. There is no future. There is just this openness. It wasn't frightening, a little exciting, because I'd made the cut, I couldn't take it anymore. There were too many people telling me too many things, and too many demands, and crying babies, and sad-looking girls that loved me — waiting for me to show up as a man.

The temptation is to turn this into a movie and cry. But it turns out, you see — but isn't that it for all of us? Again, the story, I can put it down in words, it's going to fall apart — nobody's going to feel me. So you can feel me right here. This isn't a story that I wrote down — it's a story I'm living in your fucking presence with you looking — with you, for the first time.

I never comprehended that that first lie that worked with my sweetheart would eventually take me away from her and from that simplicity. So many years have gone by where I've just kept the lying in place. Even now, even today, even these last few weeks — there's always that, you know, little — I'll give you a little bit of the grey side, just to manipulate your attention, so I don't have to be vulnerable. Isn't it hard to be vulnerable? It's like you need your mom and dad there to be real vulnerable, don't you? Yeah.

I had my mom and dad, and they were exactly what you want in a mom and dad — real people, really honest, legitimately honest, at the core of the human behavior, they were honest. It was something that was rock solid for me. They were rock solid for me. They gave me a place that I could turn to, and there was always open loving arms for me — always. My father loved me deeply — oh, gosh.

So, you see, these pauses here — and if I'm looking to give this to other people on the path of recovery, the words aren't going to do that — these pauses here. Because what is listening here right now, that's the sober one, that one can't get drunk. You can't shut down life. You can disturb it, you can upset it, you can disorient it, you can manipulate it. But it's really just the shadow of the deeper self that rests. It rests in the adventure of the choices that the spontaneity of the commitment to survival and love take over.

We'll continue the story now — talk about that young man, talk about the choices, talk about the avoidances. We'll also bless him with the shroud of ignorance. For the next 35 years, he will walk ignorant of his soul, ignorant of his impact, ignorant of the fact that someday, he'll be released, he'll be free, and he'll stand here as me speaking to anyone who listens, and who wishes to live a life of sobriety and honesty and openness, and the willingness to allow life to be pure in the way you receive it, so that you can give it to another, so that they can grow.

So it goes, and so it goes, and so it goes.

SIXTEEN

1965 - White Castle and Her

Yes, here we are, 1965 on the corner of Charlevoix and Lakewood Avenue in Detroit.

Nothing could dissuade me, nothing could change. The decision had been made instantaneously in my wholeness.

There is no fear, doubt...There is no lack of self-esteem...There wasn't anything that caused fear for my survival.

There was a deep sense — I needed to do this, and I needed to be responsible only to what came next, for I couldn't handle anything else.

Standing there, I started to walk. It took me some time. I walked up Lakewood, to the corner of Mack Avenue, walked across the street and caught a bus.

I just didn't care. I just rode that bus, and rode that bus, and sat in the sunshine as it came by the windows, I remember, and the people and the motion of their lives. People, to me, that seemed to have some form of stability — get on the bus, get off the bus.

There was a space — the space of openness, the space of looking, the space of allowing everything just to be exactly as I saw it and heard it, for my life four or five hours ago had dissolved. There wasn't a Bruce Hubbell, there wasn't a Mary Kay Hubbell, there's no Robin, no Amy, no Stuart or Evelyn.

There was just me and the bus and the sunshine.

I can remember there was a calmness and a peace that felt so deeply satisfying.

I remember closing my eyes and listening to the rhythm of the bus as it went along its route, and it felt nurturing and simple, just the hum of the engine, the warmth of the heater that was around my feet, and the satisfaction that these individuals that I was watching were just exactly what they were — the kind students that were getting on and off, the kind ladies that looked like they were going to clean somebody's house; and then the men that were on their way to work with their lunch buckets, getting on, getting off.

I traveled with that bus, saw a couple of kids that were up there. When they got off, I decided to get off with them, because they were like me, they were just a student, they were just a kid, and there was something in the simplicity of the crowd of the kids that I blended with, knowing I wasn't one of them, but they didn't know.

I looked like one of them, they didn't know.

They didn't know I just dropped a life, they didn't know.

The looks from the young girls and the boys as they were my temporary friends as we walked into White Castle and sat down and ordered some hamburgers.

The guy behind the counter thought I was with these girls sitting next to me, and she looked at me and kind of smiled, and I smiled back.

But I was way above it all — I was just watching it.

These little teeny hamburgers came, I couldn't even eat them.

I looked up at the traffic going by and the life going by…And I felt lonely. I felt like I couldn't hang too much more with this life, with no name.

I saw a telephone in the corner of the White Castle, so I decided I was going to give one of my buddies a call.

Went over to the phone and called him up, and they weren't there.

The phone rang, and I thought, let's jump on a train, let's just get on a train and go anywhere, just buy the first ticket and just go, just go.

I had enough money and I hailed a cab, and it took me down to the train station downtown Detroit. When I got in, I sat down in this mausoleum of wood and marble, and all the colors of life walking by me.

I sat for quite a while, but then, a beautiful lady — beautiful girl, beautiful young girl, early 20s — stopped in front of me.

She looked at me and she said, you look so sad, and it made me smile, made me laugh. She and I liked each other intensely immediately.

In that occasion with that young girl, young lady that I met that day in the train station, it began to solidify in my ability to live two lives.

Of course, I couldn't have told her what had happened. That wasn't there.

I was falling. There wasn't anything behind me, there was no one I…There was a refreshed space of mystery and innocence that I loved. I think it's that place, which is the true secure place of innocence; but I couldn't own that then as who I was, for there was motion in the space of becoming.

There was the event of learning and growing and interacting with what was fresh and new. There's nothing about the event that was other than raw life itself — innocent, loving, caring.

The moment of that intimacy, I remember it quite well. This beautiful lady was a secretary at one of the offices there at the train station, and our encounter was something out of movies. It was that glance — it really was a glance across the room type of an event. There was an instant falling in love and joy and the locking of our eyes and the coming together, where she stood in front of me. It was there, we knew we wanted each other, but it wasn't like — it was the, I want to be with you, I want to hear you, I want to look in your eyes, I want to see your hair, watch your lips move. I want to find myself giggling and laughing and feeling embarrassed. I want to allow you to lead me and tell me you like me, and then tell me again.

And then I'll fall away, and I'll shy into a place of — oh, you really didn't mean it, did you? Oh yes, you did. And it's wonderful rhythm of the — are we dancing? I think so. Are you sure? I want to. Do you? Oh, I do so much.

That event, and the gentleness and the sway of — No, it's the embrace of the romance and the movement and the attraction, to bond and to mate, to procreate and to continue the joy.

That deep organic vortex of committed motion of life took me over, and I wanted it to.

But there was a place that was watching it; there was a place that knew it was a lie, because I was withholding, I wasn't completely confessed. I could feel a pulling in my back and a shadow in my heart…But I wanted her joy in my eyes more than that.

And we fell together for an evening, and yet, for me, I couldn't consummate. And that was very familiar with me in many, many of my encounters that were not right.

Sometimes, I think with the ladies where it could have been right for them, and they wanted to make that commitment right there — physically, I couldn't perform, everything else was working right up to. I was full-on passion, and I just didn't have an erection. That was the only thing that was missing. Everything else was there, and I've been able to cope with that.

Today, that's not an issue.

When my relationships were full, that bonding and union would take me over.

But it's only even now in my 60s with my current wife has it started to really be as innocently playful as it was when I was 16 and 17.

Something in the abandonment, I just could not let go of and let dance itself. Sometimes in the aggression, it feels selfish and almost out of control.

The male thing of…out of control, you know?

So that day in the train station, that night in the car, the drive-in, I knew that I was a liar, and I knew I would going to continue to be that because it worked.

But I wasn't sure which part now was lying about which part. And as I look at it, there was innocence and intelligence and integrity on both sides of the behavior, the withhold of which I should not tell you, and the turning to, you may have all of me right now, so that her abandonment could be full, and she could enjoy that place in herself, and knowing that there was going to come a moment in her glance to me, where she would come to reconcile the fact that I truly was not available — not all of me.

The smart women saw that, the hurt women didn't. So we could dance for longer in those days.

Wow — just never know what you're going to find when you look at life from a place of innocence, comprehending that the story of my life is just the story of a life, and yet, there's the powerful intelligence and purposefulness of anyone's life, the core behavior that surrounds anyone's life from the time it is, to the time it isn't.

Nowhere along that journey are there credentials of authority that are greater than that one's experience.

The honoring of the intelligence surrounding the must be so of wholeness from the instant of birth, to the instant of dissolution; the errors and conceiving that there'll come a point in the time of being, where it will be intelligent enough to talk about itself and to talk from itself as authority itself.

But it's always there.

The intelligence is always there, the ability to communicate about its presence, about its wholeness, about its completeness, and about its innocence, that requires a choice — a choice to stand up, a choice to tell, tell it all, look back, tell it all, leave nothing out, leave nothing out. There, in the confession, the understanding is full — it's already complete, and it always has been.

So now, given you a little bit of a background on the capacity of that young man to love, physically and emotionally.

That doesn't mean that he isn't going to be tempted. That doesn't mean that he won't go ahead and try to exercise what appears to be a call of something wild and loving and satisfying.

He didn't find it that way.

But in that moment, when he got off the bus, walked into White Castle and headed off to that train station, there was a moment when all of that dropped away, and another young lady walked into that young man's life.

For a day, they were in love, and then it was gone, and I didn't even remember her name, but in a train station and an evening of intimacy, my life was now unknown to me — completely unknown to me.

There I rested, by myself, in a hotel room downtown Detroit, and I couldn't sleep — I just couldn't sleep.

SEVENTEEN

1965 - In the Dark — Turning Away from My Father

In the stillness of this moment, I rest with that young man who now lays upon a pillow, those hours and hours awake, looking at the choices that had been made; looking at the incident with the lady and the desire to consummate, fulfilling it without her presence...

...the sadness and the darkness of the room starting to kind of take over...

...there was a hollowness, there's nowhere to go, there's no one to call; the sounds of the traffic; the waiting for the light in the dark; ...looking back...seeing no other option...feeling a strange sense of innocent strength (not knowing the strength, but the strength was there)...hands behind my head...looking at that Valiant....... turning away from my father...back to the girl in her moment a few hours ago — I can still smell her...I could go back tomorrow, I could tell her everything, we could have a new life; but, I can't get there, I can't — I want to get there, and you saw I couldn't get there...and that's where we left it, and the tear — I saw the tear, darling...there wasn't anything I could do...you drove away and that was it...

...here I am, I see my grandmother somewhere...I remember my grandfather, I remember his sadness, and I remember that picture...I turn away from my dad, I turn away from him...I don't want to listen to him — I turn away, I turn away...I want to be angry, I want to be sad...there's nothing...just this hollow empty-looking, filled with the sound of cars, off and on, and no light, except through the window in the city:...it all hangs...it all hangs...I turn away from my father...I see the Valiant driving away...I couldn't eat those hamburgers...I'm sorry, I couldn't stay.......I turn away from my father...

::...I hold an opening; an opening has taken me over...there's a clean break...I can see the morning light now...I feel tired...I think I'll go to sleep...

EIGHTEEN

REVEALING the CORE LISTENING of RECOVERY

As I feel this grace . . . in this performance . . . this singular performance: . . . I feel you guys so much.

It's important to pause here just for a sec, you know . . .Because you can hear, it's the voice of any person; you know, it's the moment of any person; and it's that beyond the drinking, you know, to the place of the stillness undisturbed alive, intelligent, and safe and innocent.

Knowing it's simply here, just simply here that confession, the place where I reside in that discovering of those confessions. It is holy, it feels so holy, in a way of, you know, because the innocence that's being revealed of us all, the ability to be helpless, you know, and the motion of a good person, but to be helpless -- that's exactly where we are.

But we don't reside there, see; we don't sit there; we don't allow there to be there -- we dance around there; we entertain there, we overeat there; and we forget there, we are there always here.

So that time for me is this time for me, this pause for me.

I wanted to reopen up the core, what the intention is, of anyone who sits down and writes, and allows the voice of experience to speak.

Somehow in this wonderful theater, the song of the soul sings so simply, I can't help but let it say itself -- it's too obvious.

It takes over, but it's not a distance any one of us is from; it's in the core, out of the core, it's nowhere away from.

See, that's the revealing, as our innocent stillness and our intelligence and our strength.

And to honor that as I am, the place, the being-ness, as our wholeness; we then thoroughly get to enjoy the theater of the present listening to someone else's performance.

We must honor the listener, and we must open up the ears deeper and wider to recognize the authentic source of all -- of all of all. l'Chaim -- there's no other way to say it.

And it is that, and this is that.

Oh, the few ears that shall enjoy this song.

Yes, tears will fall for all of us, you see.

The simplicity of moving waves of love -- it's all this is to you guys.

As I sit here in the blooming wine orchards, sitting in the sunshine, and the passing trucks, and people on the way to their lives -- always available for a glance, though, you know.

In that instant, this instant, the profundity of who we are is revealed.

And I hope, and I pray, and I suggest, and I say this::

. . . this part . . .this part is all for you!

NINETEEN

REMEMBER - Shine to the CHILDREN and
Those Who Wish to Recover

In the face of knowing and accepting, I'm a poet; in the face of knowing, accepting that I'm an author; in the face of knowing that my words spill out of my heart and my soul, and rhyme and reason to no one else but myself, I allow this power of speech to be — I don't hide from it at all, I can't. There's nothing left.

It's the children I think of, you must understand. Enjoy as you will, but pass it on, please.

This is the message — I shall hang this story upon this word: We have a responsibility to shine back before they enter the rooms of the parties of adolescent; we get to shine back to the children, the consequences of their choices; we get to shine back to the children, so that they see and can tell us what they see before they enter that room and make that choice to have fun, and to remember to leave the room.

So in this profound statement of accountability, to all of us who listen to this accounting, remember: It's not about me. It's not about you. It's about the children.

That's what this is all about.

TWENTY

Freedom of Tribal Order & Real Joy of Conscious Growth

Be it is in the joy of singing the words that were free, so we know it's not the words. Years ago in the times before words were written, we all spoke from the heart, felt from the heart moments, and those moments were true moments — the moments of the gentle adult life speaking to its tribe. It is really that event, again and again and again. When we sit to listen, we listen for the tribal order, we listen for the simplicity and the safety that the tribal council has set in place — a decree that all should celebrate now, for freedom reigns — everyone is free. Tell them. Tell them everyone is free now.

They only need look, they only need look, they need to turn away and look.

It is in that space that all words are caused. They're caused in the great intention to broaden the event of what one sees, the depth of honoring the display of what one sees. So that to not be disabled in the ecstasy, but to allow the reception of the joy of the realization of presence, to embolden and assure us that we're growing consciously — and it's happening and it's deepening.

It's just the intention of our most conscious, brilliant, loving Divine Source that we just recognize this to be the case, and dwell in it.

TWENTY-ONE

Imprinting the True Natural Ecstatic Speech
From: My Maternal Lineage

I just happened to recognize in this—I don't know what it is about this mouth that wants to just spill things in rhymes, so I can see it coming and it makes me smile.

But the soliloquy of symphony that spoke by my wonderful grandmother.

She would do things like this. She would speak in the present loving condition of a mother speaking to her son speaking in the front of her grandchildren to her husband to everybody.

She just spoke like that.

She spoke to Jesus in the room—not as if everybody should get down on their knees—no, uh-uh. She spoke as if she was letting us know Jesus never goes anywhere, that He is present, never leaves us; even when we're separate, we're protected—His guidance, His directions, that we can always, always trust in our confusion that He'll give us the right choices.

And it really is that imprinting that I believe allowed me to just jump.

There is something my grandmother had guaranteed me. Prior to anything thought-driven, or anything driven by chance, or driven by subscription or tithe, that there is constant protection of the envelope.

God's love for us is all around us, never leaves.

There was a way that she introduced that sensibility into the space and the obviousness, and would point out to us as we sang our songs to her about our travels around her. You know, she just gave us that certainty that we were all just playful children while she continued to allow us to be that way. The one thing my father told me this: She never saw me drunk, Bruce. She would have been horrified to see me drunk.

It was that kind of condition of humility that put my father to his knees, because my mother told him, because he was drinking beer, he wasn't drinking the hard stuff, he was just drinking beer. He was drunk for three days, he was gone, and he missed a medical appointment for my sister, and she was having an operation, it was critical that he was supposed to have been there, and he just blew it off. That event put the gun of commitment in my mother's hands with a single cylinder, the single bullet; HAMMER cocked back: saying, "Stuart, you've got to change now, or you're gone."

That's how my mom was. There were edges of her that were very real, not with an edge of smartness or attitude, but clarity. She protected me from silliness, and she played with me in our living room.

So, the women in my life were strong. The women in my life demonstrated their skills. I honor my mother and my grandmother. This event or this confession and this inspection, I feel their goodwill and their joy for me, that I can bring back to life those days of the training and entrainment, and the protection that they gave me as my parents and my grandparents.

TWENTY-TWO

Contain Celebration Display to the Children

I stand up for all children to have the kind of childhood I had, and we've got some drinking stories to talk about.

What has happened is in the explosion of the ecstasy of the freedom that's evident for all of us, so therefore, we can drug, sex, and rock n' roll ourselves to death, and display it in front of everyone wildly. It's not a pack it back. We've celebrated enough now our freedom.

The adult in us is awakening.

It has the capacity in its listening to listen to the distinction between the complaint and the comedy, before the drama and the drunk, before the death call and the booty call, and the fun of playing in life on the edge of poisoning oneself.

That event is what we do when we drink and party and hang out and do that stuff. It's not going to stop.

What needs to be adjusted is the allowing of that in a conscious space of that is that, and that's responsible as that only within inside of that room.

Outside of that room, that behavior is not appropriate.

So let's keep those rooms private, not public — back off on the celebration of, I am free, and I'm going to drink until I fall to my knee — hehehe — and take my brother down with me and my kids.

That illusion of irresponsible adolescence is getting busted here.

It's a goliath event that I shall stand up, and I will take it down.

These stories are meant to be the rock in the sling of one shot I got to knock the unconscious beast of public consumption to its knees, and wake itself up as the adults and say, "I got it."

Let's change some laws, let's charge some taxes, let's get some money to pay for the illness that's all around us because of this irresponsible use of the party of freedom.

This is over now — the time of the irresponsible drinking is over now.

My life, whatever I say, is dedicated to the flinging of that sling, with the intention to absolutely take the blindfold off of the adult culture with a drink in its hand, and ask it to take a look at what it sees before it bends its elbow and shows its children how to drink on its knees.

Do you get what I'm saying?

It really is that event.

We can't display like that in front of children.

We can play with song…We can play with metaphors.

I'm going to take you to the hilt, I promise you.

Because the dedication I have to making sure that the rest of the stupid people that are being left to care for the kids.

All's I see is a bunch of adolescent adults fighting about money, and just loving to preoccupy themselves with fantasy stories that don't make any difference, they don't have an impact, there's nothing happening.

It's irresponsible.

We need to stop.

We need to frame it up that our loving communications to ourselves and our children and the things that we do in the theater that we do them and in the confessions that we make, especially around the consumption of alcohol and especially around the consumption of alcohol in public — we need to address it, we need to expose it, and we need to ferret it out from within the dysfunction, the joy, the heart of play.

So we can't shame ourselves when we've stepped over the line and taken the third drink — no, we have to contain that behavior.

Containing that behavior allows it to be in the form of what it is — wild celebration at the edge of death !

Get it on motherfucker . . .! BUT LEAVE MY KIDS ALONE ! ! !

TWENTY-THREE

In the HEART of the MATTER of LOVE

As I reflect on the incident with that young lady, I want to honor the lovely intention that we have to, irrespective of the faults of our agreements and over-commitments, that in the heart of the matter of love and being loved, there's nothing quite as fulfilling as the abandonment into first love, and the abandonment into a sense of an adventure, sense of a partnership, a sense of finally having someone who you can trust reflect back your walk with you in a gentle way with you.

It's natural and easeful and exciting and honest. That always was kind of my sucker punch.

And the occasions of times when I was made available in a legitimate way — not betraying a wife or a girlfriend — and of my intimate occasions, I must say, the vast majority of them were consensually honest, available…And outside of my marriages, most of them were drunk — honestly drunk.

There were many. And in that time of the '70s that was fast approaching, there became a wildness and an excitement that just took everybody over, but the taste of it was in that glance and that moment and that time with that innocent self, that beautiful person, that lovely time when innocence and love and the perfection of being real expresses itself — it's like a flower.

See, we miss that.

We want to take the dysfunction that shows up later on and just say, nothing else mattered — that I had an affair — that I manipulated a lady — that I was irresponsible — that I was unconscious — that I was rude…None of that — those are words, don't you feel it?

Don't you feel in the words, it's not at all about the action of whoever's being spoken to; it's really about the defense around the speaker.

That's why we always try to honor shit like that.

But we miss—and this story shall not miss the innocence in the attraction to be human.

The alcohol will take over in the story—the alcohol will show its dysfunction—but the honesty of the occasions of real life shall not be missed in these essays, these wanderings, these confessions.

Yes, it is for the ears of those who have yet to drink, that are drinking and want to quit, and those who have drank and gave it up, and for those who don't care about any of that.

This is about the unique listening of an honest soul that traveled, ignorant—honestly ignorant. Until that ignorance was released and after my own emancipation was I able to have the compassion for my own ignorance.

That's why now, as I start to share these adventures, because deep inside of there—of all my life stories—was not the typical, stand up in front of the meeting, "In 15 minutes, I'm going to tell you my life story, and that's why you don't want to get drunk again"—no.

This is an alcoholic's anonymous drunk log.

This is the soul of my parents speaking. Me speaking.

The event of laying down and making the distinction available, between the heartfelt confession of an innocent soul who wanders through its choices, and the dysfunction in the alcoholic behavior untreated—the partying's great, celebrations are great.

TWENTY-FOUR

1965 - The Silent Opening of Stillness
The Brotherhood of Youth

When I woke up the next morning, I felt refreshed, and there was kind of a smile on my face that somehow no one knew where I was. It was delightfully interesting.

I went to the window of the hotel where I was at, and it was a gorgeous beautiful day — summer, and I knew my wife was fine. It just felt like a bad argument. I had the sense that I could just stop it, but there was an opportunity now, I've made the break now. I had to open up to what was really in front of me here. Am I going to go back to that train station and get on that train? Where the fuck am I going to go? God, I might see that girl again — that's just going to be horrible, and I can't go through that again — but I can't go home.

I told her I'm not coming back until I know who I am, and I didn't. I was clear, and it was — I didn't even know what that meant, and that wasn't even a thought, it was just — it had been said and the space was so open. It just went by like a grateful break in the thinking. It was just gone. And the openness was there, and the choice in front of me was there, and I felt that. That place is part of the thread where that place of no mind, the place of — the release of the limitations of mind, for mind is just a mechanism, it's the grand computer, it's the hand of God, it's the mind of God we use to display it for its joy — our adventures.

Then we set it down, and I didn't want to pick it up. I didn't want to think anymore, I didn't want to figure our anymore — I just didn't. There was no movement in me to go to the abstraction of, what the fuck is going on and where the hell am I. The absence of no argument was enough; the space of no confinement was enough; the space of openness was gloriously dissolved into nothing, and I fell into the question of myself. That happened a lot. It happens for all of us a lot, but it can't happen when we're drinking and suppressing our freedom.

I lingered in that state for a while, but it was way too uncomfortable. I was just getting ready to turn 21. I didn't think of a drink. Alcohol wasn't in my mind. It never showed up—never. It wasn't anything. I had my buddies, and we went down and we drank to drink, to get drunk, to get in love. I didn't want to do that. So it didn't come up.

In that looking and that openness, the love of my friends did show up, for these were my home-boys, these were my high school buds, these were my best friends who knew me better than anyone. They were with me even after I got married; I still spent time with these guys. I'd sneak away to spend time with these guys.

It was that brotherhood I needed more than anything right then.

So I went to the phone in the hotel room, and I sat down and I called one of my best buds; Howie Dawson: I caught him, he was right there on the first ring. He says, "Bruce, where are ya?"

And I told him everything.

He says, "Holy shit," and I said, "Yeah."

He says, "Well, I'll come down and get ya." I said, "Okay."

So, around 12:30, Howie pulls up in his '58 Ford. We get in the car, and he just starts laughing, shaking his head; and he says, "Holy shit."

And it was back to high school. It was back to the place of being safe and the playfulness of "anything goes with you, my friend."

In the brotherhood of male adolescence, there's an honor.

TWENTY-FIVE

The Deep Unspoken CORE Oath to Protect
as Brothers & Fathers; for Our Mothers and Kids

When you say you're best friends, that's beyond all — no one can announce that.

It's an honor and a grace to feel it.

And when you've been 13, 14, 15, 16, 17, 18, 19, 20 together, you fought a lot of battles, you won a lot of wars, you died a bunch. You laid to rest your adolescence with each other, you buried your innocence with each other. You chose your armor and you set off into the world, I will go, but we'll always be together, we'll never not be together. It's just us, the brotherhood, and it's us together, and no one will ever separate us — ever.

It's there; every one of you guys feels that. It's there; maybe every one of you ladies feels that. But there's something deep in the dedication of the tribal call to the heart of the matter. I laid out my life for you; you don't have to ask that — that's why I'm here. Don't embarrass me with asking, or even talking about it again, okay? Let's pick up our swords, let's heal our wounds, let's sew them up, scab them down, take the bullets out of our guns…But let's not take off the armor — no, we can't take the armor off. The armor was revealed as our protection, when we stood up and said, I want to be a man, I want to take responsibility. I want to stand up for the blows of the things I don't know, be taken to my knees so that I can stand up and tell you, I heard you, I respect your discipline of my attention.

So I brother up, I brother up. I turn away from my father and I brother up.

It's in that passion and in that safety, and it's in that place — sacred and unspoken and deep. Deep in every boy — it's deep. It's deep in every young man — it's deep; it's in every father — the need for responsible companionship, to take on the battle, it's unending; and the confusion to what are we going to do for our children when we go, what are we going to leave them.

That — that power that lives with us deep at the core, comes up as a war chant for men — doesn't have words, but first, it calls us to gather, calls us to tribe, it calls us to single our warriors and single out our chiefs, and puts us to our knees and sits us on our ass, so that we can listen — we can listen for the spirit, we can listen for the spirit that calls, to those that hear and that spirit is spoken to those who listen.

It's in that endemic event, outside of anything that we can think of in the playful theater of sights and sounds on stages of embarrassed thought — the brotherhood gathers now, the strength gathers now, the truth gathers now that we will not be denied.

 Now, the freedom for our children is ensured, the protection around their behavior is ensured, the brotherhood is alive, it's deep, and the sisterhood gathers to support that vigil.

We're alive as that, we're deep is that — that's the core. The structure, the moral action comes from the core — the core is uncovered now, the brotherhood stands, the story continues.

It's just life in our hands.

TWENTY-SIX

Honor's Oration - LET MY WORD BE SAID - In Love

Listening to my own confessions on the edge of what could be considered to be very embarrassing behaviors, and the shroud of innocence with respect to the fourth, fifth, and sixth steps that I took twice, the amends that I have made.

I stand now as a beneficent orator of this soul called Bruce Hubbell, for his adventures are just the same adventures, the same corners everyone comes to.

They're the corners of choice, they're the corners of agreements.

They're the Ys in the road between "I shall be held accountable for my word" or "You didn't see that I lied to you. Now, I'll never tell you."

That last one is to yourself.

That profound edge of honor, the clarity of "I've done my honest work on myself, I'm ready to stand up and let my word be said and let those who hear it — hear it in the goodwill and the good manner from which it is spoken — in love, support, and honesty, to make a difference and an impact."

The opening into loving — there is no shame to that.

The opening into compassion — there is no guilt for that.

The action of loving compassion is not a betrayal or an abandonment of one's God, for the sake of an enemy unspoken, bleeding on one's lawn.

These stupid metaphors are the only fucking way we seem to be able to talk to each other. We're all each other's relatives. We're all standing.

We're all wanting this one time, let's take the 21st century and have it be done—have my story be a story, but maybe the story of a story of all our stories of just the initiation of each one have an opportunity to tell their story to themselves, and to go through that emancipation of a fourth step of taking a moral inventory and stopping for a minute and saying, do I really know what I'm doing here, have I really been responsible.

Do I even want to stop and look? Or do I just want to continue on? Of course, drinking is a really great way to keep all that very quiet.

But now it's open, see—it's open, it's open.

There's no escaping the conclusion that we have to address the love in the chaos, the love in the madness, the deep abandoned attraction to be taken over as life itself.

The wonderful stories, the gentle signposts for all of us, they come and they will come.

But there's a rest stop called "Let's stop and take an inventory, let's stop before we go on."

Let's stop before the 40 years of Bruce Hubbell's behavior and the unconsciousness around his loving, mixed with the confusion of doubt, suppressed by the use of alcohol.

Before that story begins, let's forgive—for it's all just normal and real—it's just how it is.

There comes a time and there comes a moment where each and every one of us, in our joyful and rapture of being in love and life itself, does want to stop, and does want to look, and does want to take advantage of the moment and say, "Am I whole? Am I complete? Am I present? Am I here just by myself?"

If not, is there something I need to say? And do I need to say it to whom? For it's in the motion out of that fear, is one's rejection.

It's the invitation to the honesty that will be felt immediately upon forgiving one's self.

 It doesn't have to go through the long drags of the stories and the inter-ailments of the behaviors of the dysfunction and back, back, back, you know, and the avoidance for pictures of nothing having to do with us, you know, of screens of time and songs that are oblivious to the event of our life that are covered up by the drinking.

So in this pause, that event and that sincerity in us that wants to have our plays that want to have our shows, that wants to have our listening and our speaking be accurate — to be accurate to the distinctions of the choice to play and the choice to parent, and they're distinct, and they're clear.

Our children see them before we do. That's the hard part.

TWENTY-SEVEN

OVER MORAL VIEW of Innocence Search for Who AM I

As you can hear, there's a tendency for rapture, which I'm noticing.

That's why I wanted this to be a continuation, because this is — if I were to look back on any of these guys that have written, they've written long things — they don't stop to edit, they keep moving, they keep moving, they keep moving, they keep moving — they'll maybe edit later, but no, not in the download.

So you can feel the gift of being able to allow the ecstasy to speak.

I'm just as blown by you as you might be. Because I don't have that — there's nothing in my head that says, "Hey, you know what? You've got a capacity to speak — you know — ecstatically."

I'm kind of getting that message, that's why I'm saying that.

But prior to this, it wasn't like something I'm going to do this for you. I didn't have that interest — ever. There's too much else — other things to be said fully.

Anyway, if people want to repeat the truth for themselves…Far out.

This oration I'm in love with the opportunity to stay in the bliss of my own innocence and talk from those places, because there're really beautiful things that will come about in those confessions.

There're beautiful things where all of us feel the excitement of the romance of the dance — oh my God, the music in the '70s…It was incomprehensible — 25 and alive and geez, you know, the alcohol never hit my brain.

We danced. That's the ecstasy and the amalgamation of the life current through all of our endocrine systems, through all of our glands. It gets us up, has us dance for the romance for the procreation of itself.

So these shadings and these pauses are meant to cause us to reflect, to engage the power of contemplation, to notice that at the seat of contemplation, all the wisdom rests, waiting for the language to come and fill in the blanks of, I don't understand. It isn't that difficult.

But we have to sit down in the consideration of who we are, not only from the great experience of spirit, but who we are in our behavior as human beings with responsibilities.

We need to bring down from the great teachings and simplify for our children the messages that yes, they are life itself, and there will come moments for itself when it gathers into its sisterhood and brotherhood, and it chants its joy and the celebration of its communion and the gentle social intercourse that keeps it all alive.

But it's the distinction and the resignation that each one of us wants to experience morality as nothing that we need to do, but that which we are, and it's that what we are in our behavior already, and we know it.

So the stories that I have for this innocent boy and this young man who, I know, stood in his innocence so much, but he played, and he played with abandoned, and there came a time in his life 20 years or so later, that he knew that abandonment was the road less traveled — but not now.

We're still with this young man in 1965 who's about to travel in a car — off to California he is, on the road of the search, and the question — who am I?

TWENTY-EIGHT

Night Stalker – Polly's Lament

As I prepare to continue the story
 of a young man long ago,
I sit in my car
I can't see any stars

...at the grave of a young woman we know

They said her name was Polly
...yeah, she had a lot of Klass

The horror is still here . .
I come to be near
and always remember that past

I give it up
I give it over
I can't weep at her feet
I'm too strong now
her heart's cut into my brow
Everyone will see it, speak

It's a dedication I have
to be more than I know
to be lived by THAT
which told me so

I'm fallen now
I'm down on my knees
I'm afraid again
But I can get up with ease

It's the children I think of...

To hell with the time on the stage

If nothing's accomplished
it's been a waste of a wage
that's been paid so far forward
that it cries back to us now

Stand up, ...don't break a leg

Way before the bow...

remember the children
remember they listen
remember they look
for in there, is hidden
the story they seek
to find their own soul
—hopefully, well, and well giving...

...but not all—no, not all.

For Polly was only 12 years old
that night—which was her last
...he left her here...for no one to find

Now...my alter til my last!

TWENTY-NINE

1965 - California Here We Come

Howie and Rick and I took off in Rick's maroon 2-door '65 Mustang heading south, I-75.

I didn't know that in eight or 10 weeks, I'd be on that I-75 building it, but that was unknown at the moment. We took off, like three brothers, like three young kids, and headed down—I can't remember the towns we went through. Finally ended up in Biloxi, Mississippi, sleeping on the porch of an abandoned house on the beach, got wet with the dew in the morning, woke up to the smell and the sounds of the gulls, and the cry for the—what's up for the rest of the day, was taking us over, it was easy.

There wasn't much left of me to remember Mary Kay at the moment, and really, for the next three to four weeks, there was little of me that wasn't there with those guys then. Some skill that I have to really let go, and I'm glad that I did; for I wouldn't have come to know the space of abandon into that play as a man, supposed to be healthy.

 I just can't help but rhyme—the rhymes just kind of want to keep spilling from my mouth, it's like I keep wanting to resist it. But I don't do that to be funny—it just comes in the joy of the letting it out. It's like, why not?

The exploration of the south and the food…Within a few days, we had become bored of the beaches, and on to Texas, to the town of Del Rio, and to the town of Ciudad Acuna.

That was a moment for me when the drinking and the innocence and the intersection of two people—myself and a 16-year old Mexican prostitute, who'd already had a baby.

It happened so fast. It wasn't supposed to happen at all, but if we spent the time in San Antonio, we took off south, and we knew we could drink in Mexico.

We had plenty of cash. Gas was cheap. Time was of the essence.

It's one of these wonderful little Mexican bars where, all of a sudden, you realize that 19—didn't matter of you were 19, 20, 21— if you had money, you were the center of attraction, and you were being catered to, looked at.

We kind of got a hint of the difference between being Grosse Pointe residents and Mexican inhabitants. We wore our shorts in San Antonio, we got whistled at.

But when I got to the bar and the drinking started, it was fun. You know, she came over and she was sweet; you know, something like she knew kind of where I was at—I was shy, I was bashful, I really didn't want to be sexual, but there was a deep understanding mother that was sexual.

Within a few hours, we were alone, and we spent hours & hours together while these other guys went crazy trying to find me. But it just happened, and it took me days to wake up, but in that time, it was mi Corazon—hmm. Whoa, whoa, whoa, whoa, whoa—mmm-mmm-mmm! Her heart, our heart, those moments…

That's it. Enough now. Let it be said, I honor her. And looking back, before I knew I didn't want to wake up, I wanted to keep our life and my protection of her and the joy of having el gringo mi Corazon…But it wasn't going to happen. Then came that moment when the lie and the look. She understood and she kissed me and wished me well, and told me that she would always be there, please come back, come back soon.

And off we were—off to California. We did not tarry too much, we were pretty much heading for the Beach Boys: . . . we wanted to hear.

This is 1965, y'all!

Within days, we were on Hermosa Beach, and we were California Dreamin', man.

It was everything we thought it was — it was outrageous, it was fun. God, the drinking and the partying and the dancing — it was just everything you thought that drinking and dancing on the beach was supposed to be, drinking and dancing on the beach:

IT was — everything. . . .the woodies and the surfers, they were all there — it was there. I didn't miss it.

I almost died on a motorcycle that I bought when I first got out there. I just got me a Honda 305, threw a grand down and a helmet, and got me a set of leather pants and some boots, and got it on.

Fell in love so many times, it was stupid. It's like, we didn't care that we didn't care.

I got lost for a few days . . . with my friends going crazy.

It lasted for about three to four weeks
The wildness of Hermosa Beach . . .
The cycle rides down Highway 1 . . .
Beach baby. . . .!

My hair grew out . . .
My body got tan . . .
It happened fast . . .
I loved it., man . . .

I was there . . .
It was cool . . .
It was outa-sight . . . ya know . . .?

The beach . . . !
The girls . . . !
Even the drunken afterglow . . . !

I hung there . . . !
Hung there . . . !
Hung there . . . !

Until I had to know . . .

That soon the call would come . . .
And I'd really have to go . . . !

THIRTY

1965 - My Father's Amend Buys My Trust

One day, Rick came up to me and he said, *my dad just called me and asked me if you were with me. I couldn't lie to him, Bruce. He says, your dad is very, very, very upset, and he says that you don't have to do anything you don't want to, but he wants you to call home, please, and he wants you to call home now.*

But I was kind of pissed, if you want to know the truth. I had a look at going back right there, I tell you. But I had a feeling if I stayed out there, I was going to die. It was too wild, it was too crazy. I almost lost it on the motorcycle — I never wore a helmet.

So I called my dad. He started to weep. I listened. He said, "I'll give you anything you want." I said, "Okay, deal. I want a 1966 Mustang, 2+2, hardtop, dark blue, racing stripes, 286, 4-on-the-floor, competition package, tiger paw wheels." He said, "No problem, I'll get it ordered right away, are you coming home?" I said, "Yeah, you wait, I'll order it with you, we'll go down together."

"I'll look forward to seeing you, son."

My California — day dreamin' days . . . had ended. . . .

At least I got myself some competition, some kind of adolescence I could count on to give me a dream machine, to give me a way to stay connected to my youth — that's declared my independence. "*I want my own stallion — I want you to back off*".

That message had been sent loud and clear, and there was never any compromise to that position of my firmness about my own statement of claiming my independence and emancipation from him.

The car represented an amend. It was well spent, well deserved in the end. So I flew home, landed in Vegas, and some 40-year old somebody found the right young man at the right time for a night. That's the kind of drunken intimacy I came to deplore — it only can happen in my life, drunk like that. But now, you know, I've got this wonderful sobriety, and the integration of my own passion to be abandoned into my sexual joy is secure these days. But then, it was like an argument, the dominance, submission. It was horrible. A lot of times, it just didn't work. My God, this woman had me so drunk, took me to the bar.

Anyway, I rolled into my parents' home. My dad says, "How did it go, did you get laid?" I was like, that was — in his privacy with me — it was like, shined up a good ole' boy story. "Yeah, I left her, she gave me the cab money to come here and I'm broke; now, help me out."

He and I started a new life together. It wasn't crude, it wasn't rude, but the attitude I have now is the attitude of the man's man that spoke, and it was in the tone that I had at that time — my innocence that I had at that time told my father, clearly, "I declare my independence from you, and now I need your help." He said, "Gladly, son."

And he did do a formal amend to me, to which I didn't pay any attention to until even most recently. You need to remember, as orator or not, my capacity to look back is only because I'm not only sober, but I did a lot of other disciplines that allows me the capacity to distinguish my behavior from who I am now. And also, because I've had the privilege of being around other young boys and young men and men, as they've gone through their periods of maturation and making good and bad choices.

I know those instances, and I know what was occurring. So the typical drunk-a-log is always a shameful event; thus, the continuation of these stories.

So there we are. You know, we have that moment. And now, we move on.

THIRTY-ONE

1966 - My Normality Disguise

The days, the weeks that followed, my father really helped me get a job at the Wayne County Road Commission, and inside of three weeks, Mary Kay and I had our own home down on Lakewood, toward Mack, which wasn't too far from her mom.

So she could walk down and see her mother, she could take the kids in the stroller down to her mom's. Her mom Ruth worked for a trucking company in downtown Detroit she drove down to, and she was a dispatcher. Her father drove a bread truck, and he used to leave at 3:30 in the afternoon to take his bread runs for the Wonder Baking Company, and take around all their different types of cakes and baked goods around to the different delicatessens and grocery stores.

But, 1965, Highway I-75 was still in the process of being built. In that phase, there were jobs — jobs were not difficult, this was a good job, it was a good-paying job. It paid $3.35 an hour, and that was a lot of good money back then. Jumping in and feeling my self-respect, my new wheels and my wife now back in safe company with me, and you know, a private place that's away from school and it's away from the madness; but it's got her close to home, because that was a shock, that was hard.

I came back without her knowing, and I came to her mom's door. She didn't want me in. I told her, I'm going to count to 10, open the door, or I'm breaking the door in. I did it calmly — 11, the door was shattered open. I fixed it. She stood back, and I took my wife, and I took back my life. She and I went through the reconciliation that was required of a man who says, I still don't know exactly who I am, but I know I love you and I want to be here.

But she wasn't the reason I came home. I'm still not there. Even though you might hear something in this voice in this report like there was this rock-solid guy who kind of knew—fuck it, it was a barely 21-year-old young man that had symbols of something, and soul—no integrity, meaning is own wholeness. He could not depend on his own word, and that wasn't anything he looked at. He was—life had salvaged that age, no person there. That's part of the illusion when we create stories, like we act as if inside of that person, there was a person—no, there was a body inside of the nervous system is inside of that, and then you've got the control center somewhere in the fricken brain, and that's about it.

But nobody can get that real. It's like, oh, my God, you mean, it's like, Jesus, we have no control over anything.

Yeah, because it's the moral code that lives us. It's a moral intelligent code, and that's what we're downloading, defragging, uncoding, unpacking, unzipping, unencoding, and unencrypting— all those things.

This is un—because what's here is to be revealed. That's kind the messages of all the adapts saints and sages. It's the revelation of the existing experience. That's just more of the same here.

But in the event where, now, Mary Kay and I have a wonderful home.

I got a job. I'm digging it again. I'm going to work, and she and I are connecting.

There's happiness, there's a glow in our house. And yet, there's still there's this sense—there's these—from that moment on, when I took my freedom from my dad, it allowed not only just an emancipation, but it allowed me to return to this awake innocence that used to travel.

 When I was a boy in high school, I would jump fences onto the vacant huge golf courses and walk in the moonlight—alone, to stalk the night. I'm doing that as I speak, 1:30 in the morning.

There's only the night thing and me left. And that's the beauty of it. That's the beauty of the inspection, and it's part of the revelation.

It's this revelation of the immovable who, the part that is you and me. It's the story. But then, as now the mystery is still available — it's not a spoken event. So the gratefulness of having work and being simple, that part of the rest of the restedness.

Mary Kay and I did well for months. But in that restedness and calmness for her, there had been cut loose in me an animal, an individual that craved...

I wanted the edge again.

I would find it and I'd seek out other guys that had edges I liked.

One of the edges I liked was bar pool, 9-ball — big time, Johnson City, Illinois — home of Minnesota Fats, Fast Eddie, and the real street players.

In Michigan , we had Ohio Bob, Jimmy Mataya, Little Ritchie . These are now legends of the real deal, the Las Vegas scene, and the old event of the out-of-control intense passionate thrill of gambling.

THIRTY-TWO

1966 - Feeding My Hunting for Dissolution

In '65 when I got back, I met a man by the name of Fred Kemp—Flawless Fred. I didn't know he dominated in 9-Ball down the river. He was just a quiet beautiful man—a superintendent on inspection of the line for the Wayne County Road Commission, and I was on his crew.

I was on a road crew that would set up the stakes and the grading's for the design of the layout of Highway I-75. We had our crew chief, and I was a rod man.

It was Michigan weather and it was great.

Now I was into a new life, and I liked it. By the first part of winter, I'd been talked to by the foreman. He said, "We'd like you to consider being a superintendent, think you'd be good, we'll put you in training."

So they took me off the rod, they took me off the team, and they gave me an opportunity, they gave me a pay raise, a whole dollar—I was thrilled.

I got to go to the bar more, and drink more, and play pool more, and deceive more. It was becoming more and more common, the nights I was hunting. I was always hunting at night.

I wasn't satisfied.

My wife was putting up with it.

She wasn't drinking, but there was a craving in me...

I had to go out. I had to go be on this edge. I had to always get to that edge, and alcohol always seemed to, like, snap it, so that that event with my dad, it would appear—the opening would appear, and the constant drinking would cause this opening, this freshness, and this joy, and the music, and the timing of things, and the intersection of the certainty that I'm doing the right thing, because of how much fun it is and my feeling, and how joyful it is with the person I'm with—mostly all the time without my wife.

That's just how that was.

It was at that individual who had given birth to itself…It was alive and alone and hunting.

And, the hunting wasn't going to stop for quite a while.

THIRTY-THREE

1966 - Back to MSU via a Drunk or TWO

In the winter of '66, I made a commitment to go back to Michigan State. I didn't want to leave it the way that I left it, and I wanted to finish, and I didn't want to work on this crew. I just made a commitment to get a degree and I wanted to do that — whatever that was going to take. I didn't want to be this deep in life already.

My wife was beautiful — God, she's 20 years old — not even 20, she's 19. There we are — we've got two babies, and I'm starting to get overwhelmed and I get the itch again. My cousin Michael Horlick is now at Michigan State, and he and I are starting to connect, and I'm having more reasons to get away.

So by the time that spring quarter comes, I got Mary Kay and I back; or back to married housing, kind of back in the saddle.

By end of the winter quarter, I would quit the job. I was down in Michigan State trying to finish up my quarters, finish up the old ones I left behind, working it out with the teachers.

Most of the time, I was just running with these guys, just getting drunk every night — every night, all the time. These guys weren't women-chasing guys, not even close. They didn't have that hunger. It was just guys chasing guys — just fun, silly fun, watching Batman fun, and hanging.

But I slept. I slept for two months. In the midst of this agreement that I was going to go ahead and get my courses — I was, but it took me 20 minutes to really do that. But the way I framed it, I got two months. I'd go home on the weekends and be with her, and I'd go back to school, but I was going back to the play with these guys, and off to the bars — it was out of control and it was fun, but it was just beer drinking, pool, and beer drinking, pool, running around and being a fool. That's what it was, it was glorious, I loved it — wouldn't ever have traded it.

I had my wife covered. She could be at her mother's house two blocks away.

But in the winter cold and the loss, and I'd call her and we'd connect. She knew I wasn't there. I think she was so fucking frightened by the last experience of being left alone, and now she's got two kids — she was the mother kind — she loved being a mother — that wasn't a problem and she had no friends. No one. I can't even talk about that.

That's not where my vision — that's not where my attention was at, that wasn't where my direction was going.

It wasn't just into the wildness. It was life abandoned to itself.

Still, I did the right thing and got us into married housing by June, and I finished spring quarter, and was right in there. Then that summer, I worked with her brother on construction, and that was good.

During that summer, I also met a man, Jim Harris; he was in hotel restaurant school. I just fell in love with Jim, and I said, "Yeah, let's go do happy things for folks." That turned me on.

I made the commitment to go into HRI: Michigan State University; College of Business; the Hotel, Restaurant Institutional Management School.

In the fall of 1966, I started my hotel restaurant school classes, and immediately started working at Kellogg Center into the management squad that they have — start at the bottom and work your way up — and all the practical classes and courses, and quantity food production and quantity food preparation, quantity food presentation.

By the winter quarter, I was a supervisor in one of the dormitories, Wilson, on the campus at Michigan State University, in charge of 115 people as we ran the food service to support the full-time cooks that managed feeding 1500 kids, three times a day.

It was quite the event of having all those meals, and having everything ready; I was into the swing of it, I liked it, I got paid for that, credits for that. You had to have 800 hours in order to get credit.

I also stuck my head in and got myself a couple of grants and worked some odd hours and did some research for the dean of the department of hotel restaurant school.

By the winter of '67, Mary Kay and I were connecting. Our intimacy had improved a bit, because we were getting drunk together, and she liked that. I started to look at joining a fraternity as wanting to legalize my gallivanting, hang with other guys and control it, and put it under the gentle umbrella of boys being boys in a school of learning.

Deep inside, there was something coming, and I still couldn't see it. Only in rare moments of being out of control with the drinking could I see that there was an insanity that I needed to go to.

This playful time of 22-23 in '66-'67 gave me a time of accountability.

For the next three years, up through 1970, I was a student at Michigan State University. Graduated and received my degree in August of 1970.

THIRTY-FOUR

1967 - Hotel Restaurant School — And a License to Fun

During that time, up until 1969 before Mary Kay and I had our split, the times for me were always this double-headed individual.

Even in my freedom when our relationship broke down and I was cut loose, there was still the face of the conversation that people needed to hear of who they thought I was.

I dressed that way, but there was always a deep questioning that was going on — it was going on in the searching, it was going on in the behavior, it was going on always the looking for that edge, that edge of the dissolution, because it wasn't just in the dance, it just wasn't in the drunkenness, because it was always — there's a newness.

It seemed to be validated in the music — there seemed to be a song in the music, there seemed to be a thread in the music for me that was starting to call me, it was starting to call me into the listening to the dance of it, into the dance of life speaking through and in the ecstatic moments of drunkenness.

In 1967 I pledged and was accepted into the Alpha Gamma Rho fraternity. The pledge president of that class. I became an AG Rho frat boy, married, with two kids.

By the summer of '67, I was off to Friendly Ice Cream, off to an adventure that was bizarre, strange, and starting to set a tone for my wife's depression, soon to be acted out in a few months.

But prior to that, during the fall of '66 and winter of '67, she and I were in this process of allowing me to knuckle down to school again to show that I had the rigor — I could show up and be a good student, a good father, and I was up for it. I showed up and I got good grades, and I liked what I did, and I was happy — and I drank, and I drank, and I didn't drink alone, and I drank. I had friends, and we drank, we played.

It was pretty un-abandoned — the boys with the beer, pretty much. Mary Kay wasn't included. It was just us fraternity boys.

So, in '67-'68, the time Mary Kay was ready to bail, she'd given up hope.

We got to Friendly Ice Cream, the summer of '67, I wanted to spend some time there, because it was an adventure, and there was a touching, and there was a closeness and it got close.

She and I almost had it again, but it wasn't to be. But I want to honor those times; I want to share that event.

In the midst of the drunk-a-log, I loved, and I was loved, and that's the joy of the ability of my compassion to look back, is to share the joy — not to miss that.

And I drank a lot.

THIRTY-FIVE

1967 - HRI School Award — Streets of San Francisco

We had a wonderful moment there in the winter of '67 when we were honored by the hotel restaurant school. I, as the MSU Le Gourmet: vice president, ourselves, and about 25 of the kids from the hotel restaurant school were given a free two weeks in San Francisco area by Gallo and Hilton Hotels — all expenses paid, except for your wife, that was $175.

Well, boom, $175 later, Mary Kay's with me, and we came out here and stood on the streets of San Francisco on Haight and Ashbury, looking for those hippies. Some guy gets on the bus with patchouli on, and I confront him — "Don't smoke that shit around me, dude."

It's true, oh my goodness.

But those are the things when you're not acculturated to the greater mass culture, and you feel threatened.

I stood up on a bus on the streets of San Francisco, and told some poor guy who had probably a sandalwood necklace on that he was fucked up.

So the indoctrination into the opening into the edge of dissolution that alcohol always presented was guaranteed for me. I could break the spell of anything with that; even the notion of the drink would take me there — even though that's the problem.

The drink does its job; the problem is that it toxifies the body.

If we could just free up the experience in the individual, I would be fine. But it's the downside, it's the unconsciousness, it's the toxification — that's the bad expense to the ride of the beast and the adventures.

And it knocks the shit out of our natural morality — we can't feel it, there isn't any—don't even talk about, don't even think about it. Moral—what's that? It's a word in some legal something.

The summer of '67 there we lost it.

I was starting to do a journal, and she was writing in the journal love notes. She'd been writing this in this journal for two years—drawing mushrooms and caves saying, "Hello, anybody there?" Cute little mushrooms with eyeballs on them and smiles, trying to talk to me about my penis. . . She's trying to gently say, "Hello. Fuck me, come on, I need it," and there wasn't any fuck in me.

You can only do that when—that comes as a surplus. Women have got this thing wired in backwards; that's why they choose the wrong dudes. The guys that can fuck right off are the wrong ones if you want a long-term relationship.

Sex is an expression of communion. Communion is an expression of commitment. Commitment's an expression of agreement. Agreement is an expression of feeling safe. Feeling safe is a matter of communication. Communication is a matter of intention.

That and there is where the whole fucking thing broke down. Nobody has the intention for any of that. But everybody wants to jump into the whole commitment, and forget about the responsible methodology of saying hi. I can have a responsible sexual relationship with you because you're a real person, I'm a real person, and we have feelings.

But drinking just takes that out. I don't care who you are.

THIRTY-SIX

1967 - Friendly Ice Cream Hides Unconscious Derision

1967: I was given the opportunity of an interview with Friendly Ice Cream, out of Framingham, Massachusetts. The director of operations came to Michigan State and interviewed me and many others.

They said, "We'd like to give you an opportunity. We've interviewed a lot of individuals, but we think you fit the profile of someone we'd like to have as a future management person in our company. We'd like you to come out and do a test run with us, pay for your expenses. We have a house for you out here. If you'd like to come out, you'll stay there, and you'll learn the Friendly Ice Cream way of doing business."

Mary Kay and I said, "Yeah!"

So we let our apartment go for the summer and sublet it to an undergraduate — or graduate who was working on his degree, and we took off for Springfield, Massachusetts in a VW camper bus — me, Mary Kay, Robin, and Amy in the green and brown camper bus. It's everything you think it would be, just that wonderful time of everything being unique and sleeping on the bus, and getting out there.

Friendly Ice Cream had a beautiful home for us there in Springfield, Massachusetts.

The operation they sent me up with was with a unit manager that was a franchisee who was the most successful franchisee in their chain. He was ruthless in his training. He was diligent, he was sharp, his pants were pressed, his bowtie was perfect. He ran this place with authority and crispness, and I enjoyed every minute.

I looked forward to the challenge of being there on time; for the rules and regulations, and became quite aware of the dynamics of the use of operational manuals, and the execution of job descriptions to the T, to the ounce, to the half-ounce, to the quarter-ounce for ice cream scoops.

It was how they maintained their profit, and you had to scoop it and chuck it and keep the hole in the center, and you got a large enough thing, and you had to weigh it — everything had to be weighed, everything had to be weighed. I don't want to say it again, it'll be irritating.

I finally got on the grill, and the challenge of the sandwiches, and the speed of the orders — it was exciting — and the not burning them, and the making the mistakes, and keeping it going — it was fun, because there was a rhythm. You were in the middle of the circus, you were on stage, and you're performing with a hat on and a stove and a grill and sandwiches and people's food, and the walking and the talking — it was full on when your shift came on.

I was able to elevate myself to a shift supervisor over that period of that summer. I enjoyed everything about Friendly Ice Cream, and I enjoyed everything about the excellence that they gave me to execute, and that was very, very satisfying for me.

When I got back to Michigan State, I was in a much better frame of how to participate in a career situation, because I exercised the rudimentary demands for cleaning the floor, and making sure the sandwich was correct, and scheduling people, and paying checks.

The whole exercise of going through the initial training of entry-level dishwasher to shift supervisor was very, very rewarding.

Now, the drinking. . . This guy liked to have a drink, and that's where I got introduced to gin and tonics.

Mary Kay and I drank gin and tonics every night, gin and tonics every night, and it was fun every night. And those nights that we didn't do that — not that we were drinking every night, every night drinking, drinking, drinking — it wasn't like that.

But it was included, it was part of — it wasn't like, "No, get a bottle of gin, it would last us" — probably last the whole time we were there.

But there was the other drinking.

When she'd fall asleep at night—9:00, I'd slide out of bed and take off. I'd take off into the night, into the bars, into the people I didn't know. It gave me that hint of California, and the independence that I had to be.

But I was hunting for a place to be. I was always hunting for a seat to sit, so I could allow this existence to drink itself, to be itself, to talk itself.

Things would start would start to show up—the courage would start to show up, the reaching out into the manhood of others that were older, the challenging of other men from the pools.

I took it on. I had a skill set I'd learn after hanging out with Jimmy Mataya in the bars on Michigan Avenue in downtown Lansing.

We'd close these places down, these were the hard core nights, deep into the nights I'd play until the real guys showed up, and then the bar would shut down, doors would lock; whoever was in when the bar closed was in, and drinking could be, but no one—if you left, you could not come back in, and the real pool players showed up. Boy that was exciting.

I hung with those guys. I'd never be able to compete with them— these guys could run three or four racks of 9-ball, and that was impressive.

Yeah, I was on a bar pool table, but it was still, you had to respect it.

The sweaty passion that went on in a room of 60 people watching two young guys go at it was fun.

I took a couple of swings up there, and I had a couple of drunken runs, and I had it in me. My dad was a pool player—I played as a kid.

But now, it was just the hunt, the adrenaline, and the excitement that was more impulsive — the drinking was just the thing that, you know, shut down the responsibility to pay attention to somebody else's thoughts about what I should be doing.

I didn't care. I wanted that experience, I wanted the rawness. I wanted to be where people were totally on the edge of it; there was nothing above my shoulders during those evenings — gone into it, evaporated.

The drinking was the liquid of participation. It was a fuel — you didn't have to eat, you could drink. I was burned up in the excitement. I wasn't falling down and puking. That didn't happen…yet. That did happen, but not then.

But '67 and that summer in Springfield, Massachusetts in the evenings, I'd go out to the bars and I'd drink Miller High Life — I remember that. I'd buy Miller High Life by the quart.

So when we'd go anywhere, I'd always have my quarts of Miller High Life in the cooler.

That's what it was — her dad drank — her dad drank every night. Her brother drank. She didn't, much. But I did, and my cousins did, and . . . . I had to get to that intoxicated place.

I tell you, I did not remember all this — this wasn't the drunk story I thought I'd tell, but it is true.

It was becoming more than once a week — it was three times, four times a week that I'd go for that touch. Even if it were at home, that edge before bed to push me over into the intoxication.

It was there, it was there.

So now in summer — June, July and August of '67 — Mary Kay starts to go into her needs. She's ready for another baby. She loves me, she honors me, and yet, something's not right. I'm not there.

I'm off, I'm on the hunt, I'm back in the seeking — but I can't notice that.

THIRTY-SEVEN

1967 - My Consumptions Echo the Arriving 70s

Now, when I said I drank a lot—this is '66-'67, and moving into '68 there at Michigan State, the atmosphere was pretty ritualized in regards to the surroundings and the drinking.

There weren't cell phones. Everything was, at best...

Dominos hit, I got a job there, and rode with Monahan for three years—that's where I got my big boost into thinking corporate, and our family took off in '70 and developed a whole bunch of franchises for Kentucky Fried Chicken.

But with the settling in there at Michigan State and the steadiness of the hotel restaurant school, it gave me a chance to demonstrate I could be a good student, I could be a good leader.

I ended up being the vice president of the le Gourmet club, and I enjoyed that.

Mary Kay and I were going to fraternity parties, and she was getting hit on—I hated it and loved it. She was getting a little bit more included in the rhythm, and she was ready. I'd dress her up like a streetwalker—I promise you—and just danced her. It was our way for me to just get it on, and we got it on in our living room, drunk on champagne.

But the need for the male companionship always drew me out. The brotherhood of the fraternity always gave me the excuse or the cover of classes to go hang out and drink beer and play Pinnacle. I needed the laughter. I needed the look a-likes. I needed the same mindset. I needed the same don't-you-knows. I needed the same I understood. I needed the same vocabulary, the same point of view—a 22-year-old frat boy drinking beer, playing Pinnacle, getting drunk, playing Pinnacle, chasing each other in the hall—boys, boys playing, boys drinking, boys laughing.

I had to bathe myself in that, and I bathed myself in that. I took it. I needed it. I wanted it.

Mary Kay didn't get much' not at all.

But when she got hit on at the parties, which scared the snot out of me, I stopped taking her, but I still went, and I hid.

 I brought men home, friend's home, and what do you know…

This is January 2012, right. I just found out in April of 2011, less than a year ago, that she had an affair, that's why she wanted the divorce — talk about fucking naive, right?

Everybody goes, "What?!"

Yeah. I did not know.

I was righteous, like, oh my God, she didn't even tell me. It was so obvious; it's embarrassing to say it this way and to feel glib about it. I hung my petard hat right upon that — well, fuck me! It was that place that I didn't understand the covertly hostile, she beat me at the game.

I wasn't into the place where she wanted me to be. I wasn't on the path of where she wanted me to be. She wanted a husband to retire and go to the woods, like the ones that she has — but it wasn't to be.

I wanted to be free, but not to be with her vision of me.

It was just like that — the attraction to the pulse of my sensibilities, what the true language of life's edge.

I knew that in '68-'69, I mean, the Vietnam war and everybody, the knock on the door of the halls of silence and the walls of silence, and the Mrs. Robinson's, Yellow Submarine.

The murder — just about ready to go for the imagine the peace — it was there.

Soon, for me, it was going to the screaming of the Eagles and the call of the Rocky Mountains was going to take me over. I would be born in the summer of my 27th year, and I would come home to a place I'd never been before, and I'd left yesterday behind me. I was born again.

It came true. But that...That was five years away. . .

Here I was in '67 with, my lady and my kids — we had the summer to get through. Get through the summer — Massachusetts, Friendly Ice Cream.

It's like a dream.

This whole event is like a dream, you can hear it, and it comes out of the general reservoir of that which watched. The cadence in my voice, the slow statements of facts, the groupings, the holdings — but not holding back.

Give it up, give it over, give it out.

There's nothing left that I want to shout.

I just want to be in the play of being me here today, open and vulnerable in every way, revealing my past, showing my play, pointing at the nature of being in each of us that needs to say, I want to know, I want to know, I want to know that nature of being that pulls my heart and attracts me to the dancing.

But during the summer of 1967, I was on the beach...in the caves...down by the seashore...with the gulls...and the calls of the rendezvous...and the leaning on each other without thinking about it, protecting the sacred love — and the innocence — and the innocence — and the innocence

THIRTY-EIGHT

1968 - Domino's Pizza — My Career Begins to Lie and Forget

By the time Mary Kay and I got back to Michigan State, she found a job with Domino's Pizza, and inside of a week or two, I was the assistant manager, and inside of three weeks, I was the manager of the East Lansing Trowbridge unit of Domino's Pizza. And it was balls to the walls from there on out, as far as work and focus.

And the drinking was intersecting with my wife getting tired of trying to send me smoke signals and cartoons to secure my attention, not only that I loved her, but that I was attracted to her, and I had the capacity to communicate with her and to love her and to listen to her and be with her and care for her and be conscious of her –

Those are kind of adult things; those are things you have to point out, are you willing to?

But — I live in cluelessness looking for my ass.

The story of sobriety and so forth, the fun of the chills, and the thrills of the ride are always enticing, and those who haven't gone there are going to go there if they want to go there — and, you gotta remember to leave the room, leave the room where the drinking is.

If it's become a lifestyle — think about that.

If you drink on a daily basis, if you drink three times a week to inebriation — you know what that is; that's where it starts to feel warm and fuzzy, and you start saying stuff that you normally don't say, but you say it anyway.

And if any profanity comes out of your mouth in front of your children when you've been drinking, you can pretty much count that you've already — you're way over the line — drinking in front of your children, saying anything.

So you gotta look—that's not a hard one, you don't have to go through the 20 questions from Johns Hopkins, you don't need to do that.

But you do need to look at how often do I get inebriated, and do I say anything of consequence during those moments, do I make agreements, do I talk to people when I'm drinking, do I feel the same when I'm drinking as when I'm not drinking.

If you haven't gotten this far in this adventure; then it won't make any fricken difference—but the intention is for us and the communication of the travel of the journey is to pause and to stop, and the say what's so for me.

Do I drink to the point of being different, talking different, thinking different, thinking out loud—not the ruminations of the possibilities of fantasies of virtual whatever's—but the actual saying of the thoughts in the virtual world out loud, acting as if they're real—that. There's edges . . .

The dissolution isn't that. That's not dissolution, that's inebriation—there's a different and a distinction.

You can dissolve in the dance and the tantra of life. Alcohol can help if you're stuck. It's got to be couched.

Picking up a 6-pack for the football game? Sure.

Bottle of wine at dinner? Why not.

Three glasses of wine before dinner?

You know, a lot of people would have shut this off by now—no one's going to listen to this much. I promise you, if they're drinking, it's been turned off. Because this is the conversation nobody wants to listen to, this is the part of the drunk-a-log, this is the hard part of the drunk-a-log that says, "Yeah, that's right, this is the trap you're in now."

Are you powerless over alcohol, and has your life become

unmanageable?

You see, that's the intended confront to everyone who gets involved in this Alcoholics Anonymous drunk-log. Praise Be to God.

We're all helpless at the heart of this matter.

 It's my best shot. It's our best shot.

Let's be playful, but let's keep the consideration real because a lot of people die because we think drinking is fun.

THIRTY-NINE

1969 - Our Family Starts Our Franchise

Many things happened in those years approaching Mary Kay's and my moment in April 14 of 1969.

I'm obsessed with the date. It showed up in so many other ways, so many other times, but it was a moment — it was the classic — as I look back, it's the result of the classic covertly hostile passive/aggressive, insecure, adolescent, unexpressed person having a breakdown.

I didn't take the message too well, that she and her mother had gone to the divorce attorney. She was letting me know this in hindsight. We had never talked about divorce.

The greater sense of myself said, "You're dead, and her mother helped her shoot you, and this is an ambush; they got you, it's over, pack your bags and leave."

It was very clear — not even like, what the hell did you just say? Gone. . . Instantaneous transformation. . .

She and I were over. As soon as she said D-I-V-O-R-C-E...

I looked in her eyes — I knew it was over.

It wasn't a problem. It was kind of a relief.

So, in the background behind that, she'd found a relationship — someone was taking proper care of her, and I'm certain that the woman felt love. If she would have told me who it was, I'd have said, oh darling — wrong stud muffin. Whew! Oh, well, account servicing — done. This guy was — man, anyway. It was ripe, it was right, and it was done.

Jumping out right from that place now, my life began to change really quickly in the moment of that separation from Mary Kay irrespective of where I lived and what I did.

At this time now, we're rocking into '69.

I jumped in with Domino's Pizza, and I'd moved right up the ladder. I'd moved up from manager, I was the first regional supervisor for Domino's Pizza, working with Terry Voice and Mert David. I was involved where there were critical moments of the growth of Dominoes. I was privileged to experience firsthand.

One day Dave Kolby, who was our financial accountant, came in one day to a staff meeting — we'd had these once a month, the financial accountings, and I was contributory to those meetings because I have a way with numbers.

I liked to look at it simple — what came in today? What would we send out today? How do you know? How much inventory did you sell? I don't know.

Gee, you know, you only got 18 items, figure it out. So I got us to do almost a daily break-even analysis. I tell them how many dollars' worth of pizzas, how many dollars' worth of items, and how many dollars' worth of man hours was spent today. Take that, and it should run around that business — it was 55% for everything or less.

That was outrageous that your overhead, your major costs — not your fixed costs, these are your major variables — they're handled big time.

So they're walking away with 25% net operating revenue after everything's done.

That was the attraction with Domino's. That was the power with Domino's. That was the formula with Domino's — campuses, free delivery, low start-up costs, immediate market, and fast break-even point with a high contribution to net — boom! Over — boom!

I'm hung with guys that talk like that crap; talked with the Xs and Os. Eventually my own corruption got me around guys that sold hard, sold stuff that never happened; guys who cleverly went to prison for $20 million – that was a set-up, that was a sucker punch – this guy was a genius.

We'll get to that story. He set it up and stole all the assets from two seats on the Chicago Board of Trade – all the assets gone.

The punishment: I'm going to go to jail for three years – yawn – can I take my nine iron?

That relationship was yet to come. But cooking through here in '69, and '68 and '69, Tom Monaghan had identified me as one of go-to guys with Dominoes, and we were doing it. We were going into Haslett, we were going into Mason, we were going into all the areas, and we were getting franchisees that were interested.

One of these days, Kolby comes into a meeting a year and a half into the fight. He asks Tom, "Can I buy the franchise rights for Ohio, Indiana, and Florida?" Tom says, "Sure."

That was it. There were no franchise states yet. But Dave went, "Uh-oh," then tried to get me to open up Ohio...I said, "No."

But my parents, my brothers, and I – we were starting to see the writing on the wall. We could see that there was money coming in the franchise business; and behind the scenes, my brothers and I organized some bankers, and we started a company called Franchise Foods International.

We got the KFC Franchise rights from John Y. Brown and The Colonel Sanders himself for Northern Michigan, certain areas, and to the left of I- 75. So we had all of Grand Travers and all those counties. Plus we had Germany and Austria – we were into it.

So there right around '69 and along that way, the drinking was consistent now. It was ritual now. It was getting almost daily. For sure, Fridays. . . For sure, Wednesdays. . . It was getting a rhythm to it. It was part of the current culture of the common critter called a student at Michigan State. It was the general consensus that everybody drank, and nobody thought about it – it was just the culture of the environment.

One day, my dad came and visited me. I said, "Dad, I think I'm an alcoholic." He just looked at me and smiled. He knew. I knew that I hadn't gotten there enough to say I was a real alcoholic — I was playing with it. But he and I knew what the real alcoholics looked like, smelled like, felt like. I wasn't there. Yet. . .

So in '69 and the early part of '70, my brothers and I created a company, packed it all up, financed it, created the corporation, issued the shares, got ourselves a half-million bucks from bankers, and bought ourselves some cash flow and the opportunity to take hold of some undeveloped territories.

FFI...site developed, constructed, hired and trained staff and Grand Opened up & managed eight KFC units Northwest Michigan in 1970...

FORTY

1970 - My INTERNAL CONFLICT with Men

But there in the midst of the freedom from Mary Kay and this new relationship I was having with Diane Mortensen, there was a difficult unconscious conflict in myself, and it was being animated in the relationships I was having with other men — the power inside the company that my family and my brothers started.

We'd inherited some guys that'd already owned a franchise and lost it, and now, they were relegated to manage the business they lost by someone else who was an absentee owner.

And now some smart-ass kid from Michigan State's coming in telling him how to run his business he lost, to which he's now an employee.

The resentment and the way this guy attacked me was professional. With inside a month, I hated this fucker so bad, but I couldn't — he had me. I didn't understand what and how he was doing it, but the setup, the constant setup, and I could see him smile, I could see his insanity, and I could feel I was caught, and I knew what fighting straw dogs felt like — could not kill this fucker, and I couldn't get at him.

There was something in my lack of depth, seeing people outside my box.

This guy was a professional social predator, like playing with people. I've seen those kinds of characters — it's the way they survive the relationship with their parents. They love to sucker-punch little bitches like me — and he whacked me around. Finally, I walked.

In the derision of that, and the face of these other guys not appreciating the 24/7 commitment I felt I was giving, I wanted to split and go see my estranged wife's daughter — my daughter. She almost locked me up in jail for not having enough money for child support.

There came a moment when I couldn't go down to my daughter's birthday party. I thought, it's going to be this, and it's always going to be this, there's going to be someone else — and I know what I've done, and I know what my capabilities are.

So fuck all of you, I quit, I'm going on my own. And I bailed.

Talked to my dad, and he gave me $5,000 and went to work.

So 1970, '71, '72, right up until '73, I had adventures in drinking.

Right then, I was able to take my freedom from my family and support from my father, and I went on my own, and I didn't regret it.

But, I sure liked to drink, and there was more drinking coming.

FORTY-ONE

70s The Rut of the Male FOR the Women Who Preen

Part of the dynamic of my life at that time, and up until I got out to California in '76 and stayed out here, there was an ethic for me that always kept me employed — no matter what I was up to. It wouldn't only take me a week, two weeks, three weeks — if I decided to make a change, I'd have someone who'd want me. So I created lots of opportunities for myself to stay financially stable. My father was a good resource, but my own pride kept me in the games, and I was dedicated to being good, and I wanted good things to happen for myself. I wasn't falling back.

Now, the wild bunch — Goddamn. I almost don't want to talk about these fucking guys, but I have to.

It's a big gang. I ran with a gang of good-looking, hard fucking guys. . (Jim Ball of Rochester, Steve Kuna of Holland, Bruce Baker of Lansing)Man, oh man, we were popular. I don't want to talk about that anymore, though. Not right now.

In the events that are about to be told to you about these young men and I…That created another personality when we got together

It was just that wonderful haunting call of the rut of the male and the dance on the floor, and the women that preen themselves and prepare themselves for the arrival of young men like us that showed up during those years.

There was a year or year and a half where I'd bathe myself in that male tantric dance, and I played around it with these men. We got in and out, and sometimes it was good, sometimes it was bad, sometimes it was straight, sometimes there were lies.

Most of the women knew what they were dealing with. They were dealing with guys that were talking to them — "Do you want it now, or do you want it after now? Because if it's after now, it may not be you."

There was ruthlessness to the hunting, to the attraction, to making sure that the woman you chose to sleep with that night fit your model. The selection was vast. It wasn't about that—it wasn't like, oh, I score every night—it wasn't that. It was the deep heat, the rut, the event, the constant lack of fulfillment, even when she got fucked—badly. It didn't happen. It was an organic event that continued. It wasn't eased up by anything. It was a moment, it was organic, it was live. It was a 26-year old hard-on, looking for a place to go. That's just how it was, that's how it is. It's like that event in males, and the women crave it when it's right.

You go to bars where everybody's trying to make it right, because they think the mating signifies a significant commitment. The only thing you end up with is a social disease and a broken heart.

So those times of running hard with those guys. I don't think I even want to talk about the adventures. They were rude, they were crude. They were strategically placed to take these women down, and some of them just were crazy to get it—but you had to be there, you couldn't turn away.

It's kind of like in traffic, you know, you get stuck or you try to take the shortcut. You learn to take the shortcut.

Eventually you got to pay your time in traffic, something about the prurient aspect of the gawking-ness of the male sexuality. Guess what, stud? Line up, you're next.

For a year and a half, I don't know who was fucking who, you know—God.

But there wasn't anybody sober. That's part of the deal—you had to liquefy up, man.

Are you kidding? Oh my God. Some of these parties went on for days—days. Jesus, you know, all these buddies of mine—oh my God. Not even...

That's why I really dislike all this stuff on TV—display too much to our children…It's terrible. I don't even want to ingratiate it, but I was drawn in.

It was what it was. I didn't resist it. I let it take me over. It was fun.

Mornings of regret, broken hearts and broken glasses — a sense of being broken, purposeless, hungry, starved, broke, hung over.

Oh, God. So intelligently asleep. . .

It's a miracle I got out.

There you are, you know. There's the good ole' Michigan youth — it's prime and it's rut, it's stuck in its rut.

FORTY-TWO

1971 – My Own Night Club in Phoenix, Arizona

One of the first things I did in my frying pan into the fire was to take this new relationship I had with Diane such an innocent lady, who just had a bad relationship with a guy — turned her into my fiancé inside of four months and then my wife !

Now, Diane and I took off for places unknown, with my own credentials of resumes sent out all over, down through Texas and Arizona and L.A. We really wanted to live out in the California area. So I found about 25-30 agencies, sent them a letter and said, I'm coming and I'll be here on that date, and I'll call you and you can call me. So by the time I hit these different cities, I had job offerings.

In the winter of '71, I had taken a job in Phoenix, Arizona at the Club Lisa.

Club Lisa was a fast and furious nightclub that was under-run, under-managed. I had the owner of this place called Warren Properties, who he had about 8,000 units, came and talked to me and interviewed me, and gave me an offer I couldn't refuse, and gave me my own night club.

Boy, for an alcoholic — in denial, man — here you go, right?

In 1971, I got my own bar, and it is rockin'.

My wife, Diane and I, we turned that place upside down. We took very little money, talked to my vendors, had a plan, we talked to some bands. I had a plan. With inside of one month, we were packing them outside, and it was $10 at the door for the guys, and the chicks were free.

The bands were rockin', and we had to hold them back at the door.

This place was jammed, and everybody was in uniform, everybody was hot, and everybody was fun—everybody was drunk.

I turned myself into a thief. I couldn't get enough.

The alcohol wasn't enough, the dancing wasn't enough, the women weren't enough—I wanted to steal money.

That's where it goes. It's going to that stupid edge. I got away with it, and went and bought some fucking property in Arizona—and got away with it.

Even my wife—she was clueless. Me and another experienced bar manager, we raked that place. We finally got caught when the door was locked one day.

That's the end of that fucking story.

Then I had two weeks in 1971, the fall—I got my dick in my hands, and I'm back in Traverse City without a job.

That was a quick run—Club Lisa was a quick run.

I won't take you to the drunk-a-log, you can just imagine nine months owning my own bar.

I was just—I want what I want when I want it, and I got around other people who did.

FORTY-THREE

1972 - Sky Valley Ranch & Out the Back Door

Life changed fast. Who wouldn't notice that, right? ...except an alcoholic.

But the times were violent. Geez, when we were in Club Lisa in Arizona, our bands were just right behind the Three Dog Night and Chicago—it just was awesome. We didn't have DJs. We had guys who were great cover bands—they were great.

The gentle time there with the fall of '71—I'm telling you, '72. God, I can pack some shit in there, didn't I?

So, after the dance out in Vegas area, then back into Michigan, into Northern Michigan, my sweet Diane, we enter into a new adventure for a few months, about a year—then it was over, but it was an interesting year.

But, now in the fall of '71. . . . . . . I'm back on my knees financially, but I'm up in Traverse City and I get a job as a bartender—gee, I think I can do that all right. Holiday Inn, Traverse City…

Diane's happy, she's back with her mom; her mom lives close by in Alden. She's got a sweet mom, a sweet dad, sweet people, gentle people, quiet people.

Diane loved the thrill of the ride with this—I can't even call myself a redneck—I didn't know what I was, but she enjoyed the ride.

We were back home now, and I wasn't satisfied with margaritas and Singapore Slings, and closing things up at 2:30, and getting to sleep by 3:30, smelling like cigarettes.

Within a month or so, I had a job consulting, and then becoming the full-time manager of Sky Valley Ranch: All Seasons Resort, Western Museum. A millionaire out of Flint, Phil Lawrence—

painter, sculptor, millionaire—bought 450 acres, which is now the Kalkaska golf course.

We turned it into this incredible event inside—this guy cut me loose, gave me $85,000; in a matter of 90 days, I had 700 people in it, on it, all over it.

It was a blast. I used every insight, every trick, every scheme, and the place was outrageous.

He built these beautiful custom glass cabinets for all his Western guns and Western artifacts and Indian artifacts and Civil War artifacts. They were all put out in display in these cases that he made because he's a master carpenter—he made shit faster than you could think about it. He made desks, he made chairs.

We bought complete inside of a brand-new restaurant, and I went back to some of my old guys who I knew, and I bought $50,000 worth of restaurant equipment for $5,000. We decked this place out, and we were racked it in. I hired some fun people.

During that year of snowmobiles and wagons on wheels, Diane and I cruised through the winter of fun and enjoyment, and drunken friends and parties, and campfires and snowmobiles in the night—almost losing my head on a barbed wire fence going 60. If the fence hadn't broken, it would have been over.

Stupid miracles like that—there're too many times. I can't go through the stupid breakdown drunk-a-log. I won't do that to myself.

I made my amends. I won't embarrass myself anymore with the ridiculous stuff I risked my life against, and other people's lives—that's it.

So we had a time, and Sky Valley Ranch, All Seasons Resort and Western Museum was up and running.

But again, my soul was starting to hear itself talk. There was something in the absence of the pressure, and everything was done, and everything was complete—there was nothing left to do.

The absence of the excitement of what's next was missing because now, it was just day-to-day. We're going into the spring; we're going into the summer. Man, you know, there's nothing to do.

So that pause, that place, you know, during that time, pre-running with the guy's time.

You know, it came to a halt one day.

Lawrence comes in and says, time for you to go! I was out of gas. I gave everything I had for five months — it wasn't enough. It wasn't enough I lived at the fucking place; I helped run it.

But, I was out of gas.

There was another call, and I could feel it.

The detachment to the message I was being terminated was relief. In a few days, Diane and I had moved down to Michigan State, back to the Michigan Avenue, and back into a nice apartment.

Within a week or two, I had some consulting clients.

Within another week or two, I was re-hanging with the boys, and we're starting to hang, and we're starting to hang hard. I blew Diane off…and we went big time…chasing the women, making the money and spending the money…it was rude and it was crude…

FORTY-FOUR

1973 - The Boys; Our Last Run Hard; Till
My Moody God; in Silence, Calls Me to the Mountains

But then, in between the runs, and these other guys were done with me, I found these books. I found Ram Dass. I found Krishna. I found Alan Watts. I found a reason to sit down and repeat a mantra.

So in between those runs and in between chasing, I was having another private world — this world was my world, and no one was coming in.

It was just me and this breath. There was a breath coming.

And then the nights, by myself, I'd read, I'd listen to Moody Blues, and I'd read. I'd hear a message, and I'd read. John called me to the mountains — I'm sure he did, I'm sure he did. I'm sure that song was for me, because I left — I left.

One day, I jumped on a plane and I just left. I couldn't take it anymore. I was gone to God — I could smell him, but I couldn't taste him. But I was tired — I was tired of the lies. I was tired of inflicting pain on sweet ladies. I was tired, and I wanted to run. I thought I heard God call me.

So one day, cashed it all in, bought the backpack, jumped on a plane.

Thought I'd end up working for Outward Bound. It was an adventure I was looking for.

It was an adventure to find the mystery ...to stand in three seconds, where my ability to hold two things in juxtaposed reality based on my lying: . . . I was blessed to receive a message in the midst of my arrogance — I thought I was in charge.

I'm on a beach, in a canyon, on a river, in the mountains — I literally saw the future as only — 12 hours/14 hours ahead when I saw it.

. . . . . I saw it frozen in time.

That's why I'm talking like this, because it's in these places where the words show up.

There was a place where that darkness showed up, and where that window showed up, and where the frozen scene of dangerous boat accident showed up.

It took me by surprise, for I was talking to a man in the midst of that experience, and that experience of talking to him was clear and concise and driven at the eyes.

This other part of me saw that, and now, I know another part saw both. But not until this moment could I say that — how could I?? . . . where is it . . . where's the stop . . . where I can say I look back?

It's always been in the motion of me,: . . .motion of my own becoming whole.

But, now that I look back, with everything that is honest about me, I tell you — I felt the gap, I felt the dark matter that surrounded me. I was at peace.

And . . .in that moment, a bit of the dark matter fell away, and I was to see and able to be 18 hours in the future — I have no idea how that happened.

Still a wonder; . . . like all the rest of the stuff.

FORTY-FIVE

70s OVERVIEW

I don't know if it's true for you or not, but it appeared that when I was young and a child, the days were just longer, the time was longer, and then you got to be a little older. It was longer, but a little shorter.

Now that I tell the story about those times between 1962 and 1972 that were — whew — 10 years. I mean what a change. You know, coming out of high school to coming out of closets — I am not gay, by no inference. But it was the event that the shift, the quantum leap, and the culture from just, you know, back door boyfriends and girls in pigtails, to all of a sudden — everything was polka dot and purple. That's the gap in time, but the experience seemed much longer, the darkness seemed much longer.

The place that I make contact with and the review of the standing still water of my soul — that just was disturbed by its pebble ripples. There's a scream — deep down, nothing satisfied me.

That's when that itch to bust it and jump on a plane many other times in the moment of frustration, where what is showing up is not enough, I must change it all.

But there's something in the truth of that, there's something in the surrender of that. There's something in the honesty that that's just the way it is, and every night when we go to bed, it's just that way.

We don't want to talk about that — that seems to threatening to die at sleep. But it couldn't be further — closer to the truth.

You know, that which we are, that which breathes us, that which lives us that what shows up, and allows the use of clear thinking to be.

In the face of our trying to throw down chemicals that fuck it all up—that event shows up with consistency and clarity—not with the force of judgment and shame, but an opening and invites everyone that's given a chance to be quiet, calm the demons, tell our parents they love them and mean it and clean it up—clean up the arguments, and clean up the past, be a Samaritan and forgive.

You can't be righteous and demanding—it's sad.

In the face of your own death, the arrogance—the arrogance—the arrogance is frightening.

FORTY-SIX

Allowing My Voice to BE

So in the simplicity and the fun and the play of it all, I find my voice is like an emotional oboe.

It's tuned to a way of allowing itself to have the breath of life play it. I fall into that rhythm, and I like the feeling of the contemplation and the speaking. And there's an easefulness about it, and there's a gentleness about it that I like.

It feels a little embarrassing now because I feel like I'm getting better at it, and it's something to drop into. I always felt like my voice was pushing and sharp and harsh and overpowering, and not relaxed. I was wondering, when is it going to happen for me? When am I going to get to that point in my life where I go—okay, I'm good? I think I'm pretty good these days.

But this still ability to sing the soul's song in an emotional way like an oboe still has me humbled, because I feel the combination of the essence to do, and the willingness to be, and the capacity to hold it all together and to say it like it is. So I can give it to you, but it isn't easy, but it's becoming easier.

Someday I hope I can share this place of certainty with you personally. It's on the edge of insanity and death, I take this risk. I may be hanging off the edge of the mountain, but when I let go, I float up, and that's what blows my mind. That's why I'm holding on. I'm not afraid of dropping, I'm afraid of rising, and rising more to the occasion of commitment my vulnerability in the space of still ears.

FORTY-SEVEN

My Heart In the Matter From the Wound of Love

During these years, my parents were patient. They were true practitioners. They didn't take my inventory.

Even though you hear me now as a man, they saw my youth, they saw my innocence, they saw my incapacity to deal with so many things. But the one thing they never lost sight of was their son's heart, and his innocence, and his commitment to be loving.

The forgotten youth with my parents is a sacred hall.

Someday, I may go back and honor those times my deeply; but I know if they were standing here—I do feel their spirit with me—they would say, leave us alone in our gentle loving back their son, and turn yourself ahead to the future, allow this confidence to continue to grow, continue to put it out, see who will show, fall into that place, stand there with strength—the strong ones will show up soon.

That's how it feels. That's how this surrender feels.

So the capacity that I have now with this loving, kind, heartfelt, compassion again for myself, on my journey back there. I knew where my attention was. And even though my behavior may have said some angry passion, it wasn't that way; it was more innocent and entrapped by the pulse of the times.

I know that. I've set myself free from that criticism years ago, because I'd lived it.

But in the mystery of the event of the Colorado Rockies, I was again changed deeply.

The event of getting there, I think I've spoken of before, so I won't take time to re-share of the event of the actual moment and what it felt like in the deeper depth, and all the things in my life that were going on at that vortex of surrender into the possibility.

That's really what it was, when I took off from Grand Rapids that day, and ended up on a plane; where a Stewardess introduced me to Keith Counts; who owned Adventure Bound; a very successful river rafting company.

By the time I landed in Denver, I had a job and a life—exactly what I wanted, right on time. I got my Rocky Mountain high, and I had my socks knocked off, I had my mind blown. I had myself set in a confused state of ecstasy that just said, "Go west, young man."

So there was a day that I walked away from that boat crew from Adventure Bound in Craig, Colorado. I jumped on a bus, just like I jumped on a bus in the corner of Mack and Lakewood, Detroit that day in '65.

It was all just there to choose to move. When it was right, I did, and I didn't question it.

I ended up going to San Francisco, and ended up sleeping on a beach not too far from here. I loved it here, but I didn't even know where "here" was. But it was the place I landed when I came out to San Francisco that year in '73.

I came back home, and I stayed alone, and I was simple and quiet, and I had some reserves, and I walked and I walked.

No one knew where I was, and I walked. I didn't drink. I walked with myself, and I loved it. I loved seeing my youth and feeling the strength of it. I didn't talk. I walked to the bars that I used to play in, and I didn't talk. I was dressed in cut-off jeans and hiking boots, and months' worth of tans, and blond streaks.

But, if you'd have seen my face, you'd have seen the glow. You would have seen that I was going to God again and I didn't know…it just feels that way looking back, you know.

That's how it takes me over—just in a glimpse, I see it all—an aura. It breaks me down.

But the weeping has been over, this is just another moment of getting hit with the joy that I'm sharing with you, and the ecstasy of the moment of realizing something again I didn't see that was planned just for me.

I feel like I'm forced to come up with the drugs. I'm on the bus, I'm done…

I want to go home. I'd almost give it ALL up for one kiss from my mother right now!! — I really would. Goddamn.

But just her look would be enough. She loved me with those eyes so deep, they kept my edges clear. She always, always, always loved me.

Souls that changed my diapers, wiped my nose, and forgave me for everything.

Don't think this feels bad — not a chance.

I know who's listening; I know it's on the table. I know what the stakes are.

I went to God in front of you, to show you it's true for you, too. Call it as you will — don't turn away from your soul, don't drink it down a hole. If you're down there, call me. I'll be there in a minute. I won't let you die — I tell you, I won't let you die.

But if you don't turn, if you don't stop, you're going to die, and I won't cry for you, not if you've heard me. I'm going to let your arrogance kill you. There are too many of you.

I'm just happy with the few that get on their knees, and say with a please, will you sponsor me? I had that happen, you know. It's not a metaphor from something — someone being kind as if I were someone great, and I'm not.

I'm in love with the passion of the heart — to give away its edge without pain, to show that it can live without gain — open, open, open right now, don't hold back, don't.

Find a place to go; put out the call.

If you're sober and you're still absent from the soul and the sense of the joy, go spend some time alone and ask for a sign — it'll be there, it'll be there . . . .IT can't not be there.

It's the demonstration: . . . ITs there . . . IT happens . . .!

Make me a liar. You can't. I'm already gone to God.

FORTY-EIGHT

Drifting into the Story of The Deep Opening

For many months prior to my jumping on that plane and heading to Denver, I had been lost in this wonderful event of finding music loving me and living me.

Everywhere I turned, any time I turned on the station, I walked in on the jukebox — I had The Eagles, and I had John, and I couldn't wait to get to that corner in Winslow, Arizona — and I did.

I had to stand there; I had to do them both — they sung to my heart so deeply and with such privacy...

I never told anyone. I made the move, and when the opportunity was right, both places were in real time for me, and that Rocky Mountain High experience was still unfathomable — only if I can say I touched the dark matter of God, and that would seem to be fairly permanent.

The individuated consciousness that was held in place where both events occurred, you know — I don't know.

We need to move on.

In the days that followed my arrival back, off to Europe, winding my way to come back home. I was done. Drinking wasn't happening.

I kept seeing my mom and my dad. I wanted my mom.

When I did get to New York, my car was waiting, and another beautiful lady stepped into my life, and we spent the next eight years together.

That was Judy, and I believe I mentioned that wonderful lady.

There is where the drunken stories from the start. It started right away. I hadn't drank much at all while gone.

She was seasoned, she was a pro, and she could throw it back with anybody. Now I never did ever I see Judy ever get over-intoxicated to the point of inebriation—could she hold her liquor. She was a flight attendant, and she drank with the best of the best of those boys that had the pocketbook to buy the best of the best.

I'm going to leave out any other details about this wonderful person that I fell in love with, and I fell in life with.

We knew we wanted a baby and we wanted a life together. I was tired of being single, and I was tired of whatever search because it'd run out of gas. I wanted my mom, I wanted to be home, and I wanted stability. I wanted to love and be loved. There wasn't any doubt about it. I wanted to have it be magical.

Boy, when I hit it with Judy, it was. You know the signs—the signs are all over. We loved the signs.

Within a few months, we had bought ourselves a home. Then she got pregnant, and I was on my own, and I had to create something.

I made a big jump to Travers City, Michigan in '74-'75, started a company with Frank Ball.

But the drinking was a habit now—it was daily. It was wine or whatever, and it flowed, and there was no drunken pukey stuff.

There were hangovers and coffee in the morning and moving on, but we're still in our 30s, and we've got that energy and we've got that ability to metabolize the toxins in the alcohol.

So we could run through it, and we had a lot of energy.

Both Judy and I were very fit physically. She worked very hard, and she was a very, very physically fit woman; so she processed the alcohol well.

But we were always buying red wine and white wine—no liquor, we didn't do liquor—we were wine—we didn't like beer—we were wine. My taste had moved up and I was starting—as we got into Traverse City, we started to party down with people our age, and it became a blast.

We were lost in the "Magic Bus" that I literally bought in New Jersey, and we lost $4,000 on a house and bailed on it, and plunked our ass right into Traverse City, where over a period of five to seven months, my business collapsed because of the overstimulation and lack of real planning and patience.

I wanted what looked like success. I got the building and the car and the clothes. I was a HAVE—DO—BE. I wasn't being what I was.

What I was, was just a seeker of his own soul, he was on his journey of his dysfunction, and his coming up against that, against that—which it was, it was a searching in me.

You know, everything was…I wanted the next thing, the next thing—the yoga and the book and the Krishna.

My thirst was unquenchable; for somewhere out there, I felt like the truth was going to be—it's going to be there, it's gotta be somewhere.

But, during the time that I was building Hospitality Systems, I set all that stuff aside. And when the business started to crash, I just went into doing magic mushrooms, and chilled, and passed into a whole other phase of irresponsibility because I was out of choices—failed.

I thought I had it right. I had Singer Corporation—I thought I had it right, and I didn't.

So we ended up with a condition where I was on my knees psychologically and emotionally, and then Judy had to go back to work. Fundamentally, what that did is it put me in ripe position to go to Est.

Werner Erhard taught me to BE; LOOK & LISTEN. . .
AND
<u>Take What You Get!</u>

SIDE NOTE:: to clarify my life outside of drinking . . .

As for many of us: The Est Training began an incredible journey of personal self-discovery.

For me; in 1975; I was totally emotionally, psychologically collapsed in Michigan when I heard of it.

I heard of this "training thing" from a hitch hiker, I never saw him again, who actually had not taken the Training...but he had just come from SF, I trusted him, a beautiful loving sincere person — I liked the way he spoke — what he seemed to be saying to me: So I flew directly that week from Traverse City to SF and Union Street; talked to someone for about five minutes; put up $50 on $200 fee;

enrolled in the September 1975 Training at the Jack Tarr; Hal Isen and Ron Bynum were my trainers.

Second weekend of my training our trainer, Hal Isen, was drilling a participant because he was lying...stopping, turning to all of us he said:..." what are you going to do about this ??? This is your training!!!..."

That's all I could hear in my head:...over and over..." what are you going to do about this ??? This is your training!!!. —" what are you going to do about this ??? this is your training !!!.

I can only remember knowing what was happening: I wanted to confront this person Hal was talking to in the audience; because of all of the time others were taking to drag everyone through their stuff I could feel my breathing begin to go real deep, fast and full — like I was being breathed and then my voice and more and more until there was a certainty I had to do this and I had to do it Now...finally I jumped up in the middle of the room, the next thing I knew I was on the stage facing the person beginning to talk when either Hal or Bynum stopped me...and asked me to leave the room with an assistant...I went into the hall...feeling so frustrated, sort of tricked maliciously...I felt trapped and had a full-on primal scream (not knowing what that was, at that moment) and then returned to the room to complete the weekend and the Training.

I went on to take every seminar, workshop, event and to assist for five years; including the GSLP (Graduate Leadership Seminar Program) ; with my last participation as a PTL (Production Team Leader) for the 10 Day Ropes Course (a highly structured EVENT : A deeply emotional/ psychological cleansing experience) in 1980. .again, in retrospect, I experienced a crucial life changing moment I did not recognize actually occurred until a few weeks ago...

In 1980: After five months of enrolling, training, and preparing 43 Graduate assistants for the 10 day as Production Team Leader I walked off the site at Kirkwood...that was not easy: because I felt of breach of integrity with staff...Ron Browning and I spoke for hours...yet: I still handed off my duties and jumped on a bus home.

In hind sight that moment of my life (like many with Werner) was a defining moment; a moment for me of taking my life back; from Werner and the entire community of Est...with certainty!!

5 years later in March, 1985 I participated in the one and only seminar by Werner called: "The Symposium".

Where, again in a shear moment of panic I reached out to Est on a Wednesday to have my seat on that Friday, in the front row, three feet from Werner.

On the Sunday of the first weekend Werner gave out a Koan: "What is the nature of Being of a Human Being that allows for everything to show up" asking us to repeat it continually (at least that is what I heard!!!). That exercise is a primal confront to the "misuse" of mind. I not knowing that; the Koan stopped my reactive use of mind completely for five days. I lived in a profound state of feeling alive and well and happy. I was totally functional with people everyone was so busy with their own survival there was no way they could see me and what I was feeling ; I was absolutely certain I was living in a "profound state of grace". I felt it constantly, all through my body; emanating from the right side of my heart; like a constant dripping of a soft warm fluid in my chest; as if I were falling in love with nothing at all:...I was completely functional as a business consultant...yet unusually calm and sympathetic...

On the following Saturday morning, the first person Werner called on was me. I was sitting way to his left, where before I had unusual seating of front row, every day, every session, I loved it!

I told several incidents which had occurred prior to the actual moment of my breakthrough: then Werner lead me gently through my sharing the experience; to allow others to hear the messages and the natural steps and the following moments; because I had captured them in writing exactly when I was having them; writing from the place; "AS" the actual moment of transformation

....after he had broken down and discussed most of what I wrote, so slowly, he stopped, paused, pointing at me but looking at everyone else, including the cable 10 city hook up of 3,000 audience, and said: "I trust that man"

I had forgotten about ALL THAT; until a few years ago...

On December 1, 2010 sometime in the day my life came to a stop and ended there...well the life of "Michael" Hubbell the guy on the search – which was started when I dropped David and took on Michael in 1973; as a formal way of saying to all; I must bow to God somehow and I must change – that search finished on 12/1/10

I only knew because I felt the stop of the movement of my Being at a root search and explain level: all of my full bodied awake conscious intelligence...just stopped and paused...the moment seemed to hang...I felt a deep wonder approaching from behind me: then in my virtual world I turned around: I saw back to the moment in the Symposium: I saw Werner looking back at me here from that day: but instead of him talking to the audience like it was, he was talking to me here...he was pointing to Michael then...saying smiling with a twinkle pointing...– "I trust that man . . !" I kept looking...he said it again "I trust that man . . !"...then I shifted my view from him to Michael, my 40 year old self...had the thought well if Werner trusted him then...but I couldn't finish the thought...for I peered around him...I saw myself in 1981 at the last incident as PTL, then all my time in Est...then my Training...I saw down a tunnel of standing persons as a man, young man and boy throughout my life to my little, always happy, self at two years old, looking back smiling; knowingly......everyone of me and Werner turned and looked at me here...then I got it

I saw I have always had Integrity as my core behavior: in all I have ever done; my deepest openings and failures were perfect; I saw and knew I have had Integrity all my life...I KNOW INTEGRITY was what I wanted to know about me – THAT I AM whole and I AM Becoming Whole...!! AND NOT the spiritual stuff at all....uuuuuuuuuuuuuuuggh...I felt the secular release from the theology of life

...then I felt as if I just sat down...in my deepest trusting heart of strength As My Being Complete...I have not gotten up since...and this has profoundly changed me!

Since December 2010 – I declared my intention to continue to look and listen to all that arises as my personal space of Being.

But the drinking and the behavior were now starting to become comingled — the drinking was dropping in the background, and this event that was going to show up for me when I got to California.

In spite of the fact that I could sell my ass off on stuff I didn't like, my heart found bodywork, and I became an "Est-hole." My life changed and I couldn't have been happier.

And as we know, life changes; things change.

So we'll stop there, we'll stop at Redwood City, and we'll start to camp down there, and I'll give you the background and some of the more detail surrounding the psycho-emotional nesting that was starting to occur with myself, and other individuals who were living in the question of who they were — not only physiologically and psychologically and spiritually, but just from the good old raw position of being a human being with a point of view.

That adventure, putting myself in the firing line and on the firing line, and in the support group for individuals that are coming up against their presumptions of separation — the Est Body took that on; took it on strong.

I hope that The Est Training comes back, it's essential; people need the training because they want to be trained.

It's in the word, and people look to the word — they don't look to the authority — they assume someone's got The Est Training, then that's it.

So that is a sanctuary that needs to be resurrected.

People will flock, and they'll tell great stories about their own transformation, and they'll spread the word that they're alive and well, and they've forgiven themselves for their incapacities that were natural to them.

So, here we go — Redwood City, California, 1976.

FORTY-NINE

1976 - Redwood City, EST and My Dad, et. al

Making the jump to Redwood City was one of the most fun times of my life. Judy and I were really happy. We had our girl, Tara. We found a cute, little place in the wooded hills of Redwood City. We found a life, and we found a window, and we found a time. It was a time for Judy and I.

So, from '76 until 1980 — a good portion of that — we were loving and caring and committed. We had a deep relationship, we had a powerful relationship. She's the kind of individual that showed up as someone who's willing to serve and lead and she could serve and lead with the best. She had clarity, she had moxie, she had eye contact that was full and complete. She was a dynamic stewardess. I fell in love with her instantly, and we had this powerful, organic relationship that was fun.

For me, she happened to have an ex-boyfriend that was this porn star — God, TMI. It killed me. I couldn't get out of the mindset. Eventually, I just started to withdraw — my insecurities. But at first, everything was hot and nasty, which was fun for both of us, we liked that. And drinking and getting into it...But we were both very athletic and we have the organic chemistry working for us, so that was fun.

And, now in '76, our daughter Tara is 2.

I got a job as a recruiter for Wayne Hammond Agency, where I had an opportunity to get very involved in consumer products, which it is a tremendous model of running a business. Once I understood the methodology, it was like a product manager is to a hotel manager — he's responsible for everything and the delivery and the bottom line. I really understood the model, and I was able to be very successful.

But something else was occurring.

I had heard about this thing called Rolfing, and I went down and I had met a man by the name of Neil Powers. I had a Rolfing session, and it just changed my life. As soon as he touched me, on my way home, I instantly chose — I must do this for the rest of my life. It was just so clear to me, and the way that he treated me, and the loving way and the concern he had for me in the — not just the power of his hands, but he was removing my tissue off my bones.

That's what Rolfing does — through the intercostals of the ribs and down everything.

When he did my chest, something popped — literally, I could hear it crack on the way home. It scared me, but I actually felt like a release, like some kind of armor had just been busted. It was frightening at first, because the amount of air that I was feeling in my lungs and the freshness of it all, and the lack of concern and the tears that came in the moment of the release — it was scary.

But I continued to take Rolfing and I got involved in bodywork deeply.

During that time, Judy was working for American Airlines, and she was doing well, and flying a minimal amount of days and was working for us. She wanted me to support my heart, because during that time in '76 when we were still hanging after the failure of the business in Traverse City, I tried to get things going in Chicago, and I just didn't have the fire.

But now Judy could see in my eyes, she could tell the passion in which Rolfing had changed me. Now, I was in the throes of discovering what it is that I needed to do to become a Rolfer.

I did everything I needed to do. I got my massage certificate, and I fell in love with Paavo Airola and his How To Get Well book, and the principles that everything he did was about cleansing and vitamins and nutrition and massage. I really got to understand the organic frame of the living condition of life called human, and the nine systems, and the fact that we're nothing more than a mineral deposit machine with tributaries, and if we don't keep the tributaries clean, it clogs up and the damn thing shrivels up and dies, or you blow out a section of the tubing — it's really that crude.

We have to keep it in the sun, and we have to give it fresh enzymes in order for it to metabolize the minerals, and get it into the bones, and replace the structure before it breaks.

And the oils — everybody's fat freaked out — it's not true. You've got to have the right kind of fat. You need tons of omega three fat.

So these things were starting to become clear for me. It was like a big puzzle, and it was starting to fit together, and was happening slowly. But I could feel the legitimacy of the discipline of healing — and I liked it.

In the meantime, I had immediately become involved with EST. I started to take EST seminars: About Sex & About Money and About Relationships. I got involved with wanting to be involved with guest lectures, and I started to become an assistant, and I was assisting a lot. I was down at the center in San Francisco a lot.

I helped and assisted in the EST training. I wanted to go back — I wanted to watch that experience, because I had this monstrous breakthrough in '75.

There was something — there was an authentic challenge, because everything that came up was just like, what the hell, what does that mean? But the fact that you could look over and someone else knew what it meant, it gave me an excitement — like there was something available in the trustworthy arms of others that I'm with.

So when I saw guys like Landon Carter and Ron Bynum and Roger Dillon, individuals that showed me and demonstrated for me the incarnation of leadership and the management of my attention, and they gave me an opportunity to interact.

Drinking was like, it wasn't there — it was around.

But now, I was fascinated because I had my attention riveted, and there was an enfoldment that was tearing me up, that I was — and I'd go out in the world, and people would go, oh my God, you've taken The EST Training. "Well, I appreciate the fact that you've shared that with me; and yes, I understand your communication" — I mean, I was like a fucking robot. People just like, "Oh my God, can you not talk that way, please?" What way? I didn't understand your communication.

I mean, it was like, oh my God.

Because something had snapped, and I took what they gave me — what they gave me was to say this, then say that, now say this, now feel that, now look at this, now look at that, now look at this, and look at that. I'd been taken down to screaming, and I can't understand, you know — you'd think I'd run.

Anybody who hears that story goes, "Oh my God, did you go to the doctor? Did they give you a prescription? What was it like?" No. It was like — bam! — and it was over faster than it had occurred, and the clearing of its absence was refreshing because I was going, like, "Whew, damn!" But I didn't say that — but I was in that event of wow — because it wasn't like there was a me going like, check that primal scream out, bitch, you want another one, lay down.

No, it wasn't like that. There was nothing, there was nobody there. So when I got involved…I was drawn up, and I was reconstructed. I was given disciplines, and I was given challenges, and I was given agreements, and I was given time.

I was given an opportunity to serve other people — oh my gosh. I looked around I mean, I felt like I was an unusually peaceful person. I didn't know that, but people's stories were horrible — really got hurt, and you could feel it in them, and it was hard.

But the glory of being with them when they pushed through, and when you had a guy who stuttered: . . . who stood up and spoke in front of everyone in a communication workshop — spoke clearly with not a stutt.

We went wild when he did that.

He allowed an event, he allowed himself permission, he allowed himself to be safe — and he spoke like an angel.

We came to our feet, my God. We knew this man, he'd been around, we'd all been around — classic stutter, this sweet boy, I didn't pay any attention to him afterwards.

But the event — this life-changing event that you just can't shake the quality of it, and you gotta go back.

So, during the time with EST in '76 and '77 and '78, '79, there was a focus and a rhythm, and there were friends and relationships, and seminars and seminars and workshops and events — wow.

I took a couple of swings up there with Stuart Emory — he was another guy who was involved in this event during the '70s, right up to the '80s there, and a bunch of other people that were trying it on, hung out in Mill Valley.

It was interesting — was drawn into it — got deeply involved.

And a guy was a channel — Kaskafayette — Don't get me started. But it was an amazing experience, where you had a guy who was basically a bio-feedback tech, who got himself so damn far down into Alpha that he started to download like Seth — but there was master Kaskafayette.

We're all just like, wow — we're gone.

Because there were no repeats, it wasn't a rerun — there's nothing, there's absolutely nothing like the experiences that I was having — it was all new, it was constant dissolution of any attempt for belief, you couldn't keep it together.

The staggering fact that the happiest place you could be is — I don't know, no…I don't know.

And in that — I don't know — it was easier, comfortable in the looking from I don't know, and you get to see it's faster…Because it's sometimes not even in the space, it's in the communication that we get fucked up with — that people describe life inappropriately and inaccurately.

We have to kind of shake our heads and say, "What did you just say to me? That's not right."

And people talk like that—people of authority talk like that. There's this presumption of separation in the way the whole world works and is working.

But there's some lack of groundedness, because the fear is endemic, in the Bedouin cultures. We can't get away from the fear that our cousins are going to kill us.

The event of the opening up to the innocent damage that being born and having parents and living does, to fuck up the confidence in an individual that they're free. The EST training was disarming all that, and just breaking us through, and the excitement of the breakthrough just kept you coming back.

I was doing bodywork, and that was growing like crazy. I was getting clients that were in EST, and I was getting a momentum going with my muscular hygenics, and starting to do seminars— my own seminars—where I had a Body Consciousness Intensive— 12 separate events throughout the day that allow an individual to come to a conclusion of what muscles work for them and which ones don't. This was what was going on, this was my life; this was the bloom of the event of my feeling like I've got it together.

In the midst of that, my father dies.

That was a very uncomfortable, but quick, event.

He went in to get some new veins put in his legs because his buddy, Sam Platt, had it done, and he never got out. My last vision of him wasn't good. He was on a breathing machine. It wasn't good. They had supposedly done something with his legs, which I'm just not going to allow there, and it wasn't good. I took my mom to the airport to get my sister, and there it was—the phone call came.

My life changed.

My mother and I got deeper, and my sister and my mother and I got deeper for a moment, but then my sister moved away, and it was a long stretch moving away. She was moving deeper into her own, becoming senior, and our belief systems were staggeringly different. She'd watched the failures and the lack of the support from my ex-wife and the children, and she felt lost in that family network not being delivered. She resented me for that, and she couldn't hear anything that I was saying, because what I was saying was all new, and it sounded like jargon and crap. She was scared, and she disconnected, and she never reconnected. We stand there — this today.

We had a couple of close drive-bys, and the wonderful reaching of making contact during the final years of my mother's life. But it didn't last, and it wasn't sincere, and she was hiding as she always had for the past decade or so. That derision and that false front — the two-sided person that you don't know what's real — I can't live in that space, especially when she's my dear sister. She and I, just like with my brother and my other sister and my other brother — the only way I look at it is, 93% of the time, we had it awesome. The last 7% just happened to be the last 7% of our lives together, and that's it.

I got the 93%, thank you very much. That's all it is for me.

That's a way that people can either dip into the 7% of what was lost — and fuck that — and dwell on the make wrong and the transference of the guilt of unhandled business today.

But that isn't going to do it.

What's going to do it is people work on themselves, and humble themselves, and say I don't know, and sit down and be quiet, and allow the spirit of your own good sense to slow you down from the distraction of the transference into the TV, and the false experiences of love and hate that are just being acted out by people in scripts and celluloid and transparent digital stuff that's like cartoons — unreal and inappropriate.

It steals our life.

So in these times, during that time, there was a deep growing, there was a deep feeding, there was wisdom around me.

As I approached 1980, the demand for money and the disconnect with my wife — she was starting to wander, and she was going back. Because of her insecurities, she basically worked her insecurities out in intimate ways — and not with me. It was the way she handled her frustration. She was comfortable, because she got the release that she needed, she got the validation that she needed. She got the certainty that she was cool and she was attractive and everything was fine, because I was starting to...I was in the midst of still the denial and the toll of that on me — and I was still, we're in 1980 — hell, I'm still another 25 years away.

But there we are, Judy and I, the wheels are starting to come off. I'm hanging with EST, the body work has kind of come apart a little bit, because a good portion of my transportation to and from Michigan was being shut down.

In '79 my bodywork practice got too lean and there wasn't any income, and Judy resented it.

I went out and tried to find work. The only thing I found was one of my clients had a business I jumped in and I got on board as a partner. I borrowed money from my mom out of the estate that we had. It wasn't much.

But my mom was very smart. She was an intelligent investment lady. She created and ran the Grosse Point Women's Investment Group. This woman know how to track, she knew to watch fixed costs, variable costs, operation expenses, what was the new contracts on the table before we invest in these guys — she was a sharp cookie.

She had all of it going on.

By the time my mom retired, she was well off, and she had an income off my dad's social security and her own. She was good — she was able to make that cash flow and put a little away every month — so that her life, now that my father was gone.

But the drinking had fallen in the background.

This is '80, and now, I'm starting to work with these guys, these friends of mine, and we catch a wave, and we start to open these distributorships to the golf courses of the Sea- plant extract product. It was very successful very fast, and I was trained well, and I opened up 22 operations that were buying $6,000 worth of product, and we were on our way. Little did we know that within a few months, the Seaplant product — because it was organic seaweed, blows up in the heated warehouses.

Now we've got a big mess and a lot of cancelled orders and buyback — and now, we're upside down financially, and I'm out of an income.

So, now in 1981, I got my wife — who has now moved in with a new friend; my daughter — I've lost her; my mom is still — I could always reach for her, but I didn't.

In the midst of it, there was a horrible moment, and for a week or two, I just hung in the mystery — what the hell was my life going to be about?

There wasn't any job on the horizon — my partners had decided to execute me without notice. They said, "Here, we'll give you a couple of hundred bucks a week," and I went, "Jesus Christ, man, I just dropped $10,000 on my side to go out and get you the 22 accounts — now, I'm gone without vote?"

It was horrible — it was a bad, bad moment in the fall of '81.

Then, Adi-da Samraj showed up in the form of Bubba Free John.

That is a whole other event.

Adi Da Samraj – Bubba Free John –TOOK ME OVER & never left !

FIFTY

1981 - The Approach to the Guru

So out there in California in 1981, I was about to meet my guru, and—oh, brother, man, the stories—they're just, you know, guru? I have a guru? Now, I'm telling you, 30 days before that, I couldn't have told you what the guy's name was.

But in the fall of 1981, I had an incident, and this is where this tendency to go into reverie is going to just take me over, because I can't not do it ! These are living relationships. This isn't a lecture— giving you my summary of bibliography of someone else's bibliography.

This is the raw.

God, I hope everyone else has an opportunity to be as raw, but this is a privilege—this is a passion, this is a sacrifice, this is difficult.

I gotta pony-up HERE, I collapsed like crazy today. I thought, God, I can't do anymore — and I felt embarrassed and weak. I've been up all night.

I'm going to punch it down here, and I'm going to feel into this consideration regarding Adi-da Samraj, because it took my life over from 1981, and really didn't let go of it until 2001. I want to speak around the context of that relationship. I want to hold that relationship in my speech with reverence and respect, and it may take quite a few minutes.

If we're going to talk about the drunk-a- log, I'm not just going to take you down to the streets of San Francisco, and have you lay down with me when I did it. Big fucking deal. . . I did it consciously as an intelligent drunk.

My life wasn't collapsed, and I wasn't lying there because my box was stolen — it wasn't like that at all for me.

It's like I'm a high-class drifter, you know. Shit.

Anyway, the fall of 1981 — in the pavilion at the sanctuary of the mountain of attention — Cobb Mountain, Siegler Springs — my life was taken over in a way I still have no comprehension of how it was even possible.

I'm going to leave the conversation of the deeper relationship with Adi-Da Samraj.

The way alcohol was used around him was always for the intention of getting drunk; it wasn't the, "Let's have a Beaujolais with the chateaubriand" — fuck that,

it was, "Let's get loosened up, just break your attachment to what your fears, and some of you single guys and single girls that want to get it on, give those two an extra shot first." ...those ones that were disabled.

And it wasn't that silly. He knew, because not everybody — there wasn't like that.

These were individuals of thought; these were individuals approached because they were touched by an event — they were touched by an event that was outside of their thinking. They were touched by the destination they were to have — same in my case, where the intention for each one of our lives should be given over to that which was worthy…In a scene…that was earned…not like a badge.

And, to be devotee of Adi-da, it was a fine line between the gone-to-him and the loving service, and the pullback in the world — but they were equally done, such that all of those that felt that — and kind of had that ability to be juxtaposed — that intention to lie and separate was used up. That need to be safe by lying was used up by someone who played in the realms of lying and said, "Watch the string now." It isn't about the dance, it isn't about the divas, it isn't about the dicks, it isn't about the don'ts — it's about the event of your watching that I'm more like you than you are.

That was his call to us — the unbelievable inference in his making that very statement — that he was more we than we were.

What he was saying is he was free, and we weren't, and he was, and we didn't know — and that's what we wanted, and that's why he was there.

We knew that — we could get the abstraction because he said so, but the complication was in the fact that there's no one that could dance the word in the spontaneity of it all like Adi-Da Samraj in our life. He was free.

We wouldn't let him get entangled. We gave him everything. We gave him money. We gave him houses. We gave him property. It didn't come like that.

This wasn't a Rajneesh event; with Mercedes and young girls being taken advantage of — it was nothing like that culture.

Adi-Da Samraj was lost in his ecstasy for only those who cared.

FIFTY-ONE

Adi Da Initiation of Release into my
Vocal Serious Social Communication Destiny

By some grace that was gladly taken in the moment, I became his devotee, and I did in an instant of sexual charge that took me over. It's right there in The Bodily Location of Happiness talk in November 28, 1981. It's on tape, it's on YouTube.

The moment was there—if you want to go see it, my life was there. It's still there. You can listen to what I listened to the first time I listened to him in person—it's there.

And as I sat in The Pavilion for the first time, as I sat on my ass at The Knee of Listening. I was taken over again, but this time, I was humbled so deep, there was not a…My fuck was about to be removed completely.

There was going to be nothing left in my—sad to my new partners' discovery, but that which was avaricious, that which was predatorial…That which was defined by fear was about to be dominated in a sensual and sexual way that I had no comprehension of what it was in the moment as I sat on that floor, waiting for Bubba to show up.

I had never been in a room where 300 people—men to the right and women to the left, with a huge Dias in the front, occasions of flowers almost seeming to move when he moved, I do not tell you that. There was a stair step effect with a chair—long, wide, full seat, covered neat material, the seat was maybe 3' wide and 2' back, well upholstered.

It was his seat. It was the only seat.

When we waited for him to come, I had no apprehension and no comprehension of what I was about to see, what I was about to feel, and what I was about to disappear into, and not to ever come out.

I've never left his enrapture of me.

It became me now, for only I hold the great visions of our play, and therefore, means nothing to you. But deep in the mechanics of the very way I present myself, there's a pace, there's sincerity, and there's a Siddhi of Serious Social Communication.

Deep behind all the things that I tell you, it's greater than that.

I learned in that meeting and that day and that moment that there is was an initiation, and a revelation more than I have, you don't. It was you are, I am, you I am.

That event, that realization, that core disappearance into the living conversation with no mind — except at the times it's needed.

That place was danced for 20 years in a way it kept me entranced. It kept me enthralled, it kept me moving through all the real feelings of fear, sorrow, anger, boredom, doubt and discomfort — irritable, restless, and discontent.

There was never a time that the edge is the reality of death, but the turning to the joy of the living event of the divine person — was always there — he said it was always there.

He told us, "Look at me, do you see?"

I hope you who are listening, the vision that you can see — what was he talking about you see.

Adi-da is gone, the message isn't gone.

The question remains, what do you see and who's looking? The ability to speak that with clarity and wonder is only held back by the lack of amends.

In this chapel of my heart; in this confessional of your listening:

I'm doing my final amends for me. I'm hearing the privilege to be who I've been, to honor my courage to have taken a risk back then — but I'm not done at all. You've heard me shout — yeah, I'm not done at all. No, there's no way you're going to get me out, because there isn't a winner, but there are those who lose. They lose because they're lost, but it's only because they didn't choose.

So now we see their dilemma, we feel their concern…But it's their responsibility for them to turn. When they turn, we will show them. We will show them the mirror, we will tell them we've stood there, and we know that they'll fear, but the fear will pass quickly, and never for those we turn away from the mirror and run for the shows.

But those of you who stand there, the image will dissolve, the clearing will show up in front of you — and then, you'll know that you've evolved to a place of your choosing, for you caused this moment to be.

It's always just been you, . my darling . . .there really isn't: . . a ME.

FIFTY-TWO

1987 - Critical Moments BEFORE the First Drink

In 1981; during my first few months on staff with the Adidam community I met Joan Felt . . .instant love and caring: we created a common law marriage. . . . to included her sons Will, Robby and Nick; who was 2 months old at that time of our initiating our life partner marriage commitment

I had been in Adi-da since '81 and, you know, everyone was cool there.

What would happen, right ....that would trigger my alcoholism ?

For six years from 1981 to 1987 our family unit of Joan, me, Will, Rob and Nick; we were very grounded and simple . . . a time of us all growing up together: years of videos and laughter and closeness...my daughter Tara came and lived with us for a time

...BUT...

What would happen, right?

This is also critical, because you wonder what happens to a gentle soul like I know I was, and am...Exposed to all the wisdom that appeared prior to drinking.

What would occur that would click me permanently into my last alcoholic run that basically would last for 15 — nope, 18 years, before the last drink?

What would do that? What would trigger — because I was doing fine.

In 1987, I had had an opportunity the previous year to take all of the resources and the support of my mom, and I was semi-recruited by Microsoft.

I had seen the coming age of computers.

And myself, as a cash flow specialist, someone who worked diligently for very accurate cash flow projects, you've got to do the assumptions about where does the money come in.

Most people, they go buy shit. I need a garage, I need a desk and a computer — all of a sudden, and you're out of money.

You've got to sit back, you've got to create your plan, do your cash flow before you do anything — before you even get the computer, if you don't have one. If you don't need one in your life, don't get one. It's not essential.

Now, in that event in 1987, I had developed a skill set — I became a Microsoft Excel exceptional developer.

So Microsoft just sent me a letter, invited me to participate in the start-up team. We were a team of guys that had particular product concepts that we'd take the open template system of Excel, and create for people different things they could use immediately.

For me, I saw an opportunity in calculators. I thought all sorts of calculators, because I had been using the HP12c when I was doing loans and leases and mortgages, and that was the way I was able to figure out interest rates and payments and rates and terms. So I created these calculators that were multifaceted. I won't go into that detail.

Less than eight months after the concept, I was on the street, and I was selling, and I was selling hard. The fall of 1987, by November, I had 80 accounts — 40 in California and 40 in Michigan, because I'd parlayed the product and I squeezed Microsoft for the support, and they were doing it.

A bunch of us guys got some real cash out of them. They saw our aggressiveness, they wanted to support us, and I got lead into Broderbund. Broderbund gave me their whole account list. There's another company at that time, it was called Bonsue and they too could see that I had an angle…

I was going after the accountants, the CPAs, and the people that didn't know how to use Excel, but immediately, they could do all sorts of things. I gave them cash flow templates — I was giving them like 60 templates. I built them all, put them in a package, put them in software, put them in a hard package, and got distribution.

By the fall of 1987, I had a $15,000 order from Broderbund. I was on my way. I was pumped, and I knew I had an angle on a market. I promise you, I still got an angle.

Who cares? Right now, you know, I gotta a job to do, which is finish this thing.

But 1987, like I do, I did my marketing, I did my work and I was on it. I was low capitalized, but I went and I played with the big boys, and they respected me because I came prepared. I stood up there and I brought in accounts.

Over the next three years, I did about $250,000, and I spent about $260,000, but I was going for it. But I didn't see that in there was a change of the marketplace and the software development, that all of a sudden, there's going to be another competitor to the Mac, and it was called PC.

Now I was out of the pocket — and I had the right product, but I had the wrong operating system — and now I was in trouble, because all my market, all the people I wanted — all the accountants, all the CPAs, all the real estate guys. All the guys who wanted to crank these numbers and get those answers fast, they were on the PC side and I had a Mac product. And now, I was screwed, and I didn't have any more operating capital.

So now I had to go out and kind of try to squeeze people, and I found myself a couple of smart guys, and sold them a part of the company, and sold some site licenses, and got myself about $50,000 and went back at it.

But I was still short on product, and I couldn't really make the jump, because the GUI part — there wasn't the Microsoft Visual C++ to start to develop it. It was a primal gooey language that hadn't been invented yet. We were still back in the DOS operating language, and it was clunky, and you couldn't get the Excel look over to the PC, because the PC Excel hadn't developed quite well yet.

I was kind of stuck—and I was in the right product in the wrong market, wrong time. And I got screwed.

That took me to '92, and that fired up my drinking, because I could see that ship was starting to list, and I couldn't stop it. I even had Scott Cook of Intuit, who called me at the right time, and I arrogantly said no, and I should have said yes.

But I still owned the product rights, so fuck 'em all.

He tried to do a deal, and he tried to snap me on the product and take it away and buy me cheap.

I wasn't going to do it. I didn't give a shit if he owned Intuit. When I got a little arrogant with him, he cut me off.

That's kind of how inventors are—they get insulted, like they think just because they're going to give you the grace of talking to their stupid engineers that are trying to tell you—oh, anybody could do that.

I'd about smacked these two little bitch boys who thought they knew who they were talking to. I'd taken years to develop that product concept; still going to go out and eat their lunch one of these days.

Anyway, a little pissed about that, but who cares?

In '87, I'm starting at run, and I was fairly sober—but then it happened.

Somewhere in the intention and the destination to go to Michigan, because I knew I could develop product lines out there, my mother was out there, and we had connections out there, and I knew the territory out there.

My daughters were out there, and I wanted to see them !!

They were 21 and 20, and I wanted to see them. I needed to see them.

It's a difficult time, a lot of cross-communications, mixed messages. But, it'd been a long time since the summer of 1973. Those girls that had sat in my lap — my beautiful 9-year old, Robin, and her 8-year old sister, Amy. There we were. You know, I can't — I will never — I include that moment.

There I was in '87, knowing that I was heading to Michigan. I decided to take the risk and whatever I did on research, I was able to find Robin. I let her know I was coming, and she wasn't quite interested, but I found out where she was. She'd been — just given birth to my first grandson, Max. So, they were living in an apartment in Lansing. I hadn't seen her, didn't know anything about her.

When I got my plans set up — because I'd set up a route that I was going to go through and go to. As I developed a business model to include, at that time, independent software companies — like ma-and-pa software — they had all the different products on the shelves, so you had all these little — and these were the distribution units for Bonsai, Broderbund, and I had these guys. I called them up, and I got the healthy ones. I knew how to cherry pick. I knew the ones that had money, and I told how much it was going to cost, and I had a pre-sale, and I gave them exclusives so they'd get a territory. I knew how to segue people that way — I give it to you — and these people, their competition were within blocks — everybody had a software, and everyone was jumping, everybody thought they were going to get rich. It'd only cost them $10,000 or $15,000. They thought they could make the jump from the factory and get out of the rut — didn't happen. A lot of people went down, spent their money and that was it. Egghead took over for a while — and everything went male. Now, look, there's nobody — hardly find software packages anywhere.

Anyway, there was a big window of opportunity — a time where there was mass distribution — and I took advantage of that window when I was in that window.

I knew I was going to be able to be in Michigan for quite some time, and I want to talk about this joyously — fuck being sad about it.

This is the option we had. I was just telling my wife a part of the value of the drunk-a-log here is to go back and you look at the dark spots, but do not miss the light.

Robin and Amy and I had marvelous, marvelous moments of loving and aloneness and caring and freedom, privacy, security, abandonment into our innocence with each other. Have you ever spent days in that? And they loved it, away from their mother. And Lee, Robin's husband, we had fun — but, you know.

Anyway, I get there the first day, and I kind of hunt Robin down, and go over to the door and I knock. I could tell she was happy to see me. We took it slow. She had the baby, and we took it slow — we've always taken it slow. We haven't really been able to get to the hug on the couch again, even now, but it's coming. She's on the other side of those rooms, and I want to make it available for her to take that first step. I allow what sadness is left in me to stay focused on the mission. I can't go back; there is a wound — it probably won't heal until they're both sober — so my vigil.

There in 1987, when I found Robin, and she and I went to my favorite places that she went and I did — it's called Beggars Banquet, it's downtown East Lansing. It was one of my favorite hunts. I was actually there the day they started that place. It's a great eating establishment, and they had a lot of great food. I had a lot of wonderful meals with a lot of wonderful ladies, whose names I don't remember, in that restaurant. It was beautiful. Women felt elegant when they were taken there, and it was fun to allow women to feel happy — damn.

We went there, and it was fun. But on the way, she says, "I'm going to call Amy and tell her to meet us there." But she doesn't know I was in town. She says, "I'm going to tell her to meet me there" — meaning Robin.

There we were, and Amy comes in. She hadn't seen me for 13 years. When she said to me later, "Oh my God, you look so much like me."

There it was, and then she just started to weep and to fall into my arms and say, "Just hold me" — and I did.

There was a closeness starting to connect, but it was just starting, and there was still so much, and there was still so much energy. We were so much like each other, and there was this impulse, and we just said, "Let's order a bottle of wine"....

— THERE it was...!

I can't tell that to anyone else, and have them know what was happening.

My daughters — 13 years...?

I hadn't declared myself an alcoholic; I hadn't been drinking.

But right there, the intensity of the moment, and the joy and the sadness — there was something about the cut of the alcohol that dropped us back in our bellies, allowed us to reach out and hold hands and not cry — laugh, and tell jokes, and find out how similar we were.

I'm not going to — you got it, right? You can feel that. It's there in all of us when we fall back and love, and trust opens up.

But it wasn't to last . . . The drinking got out of control, and it caused us to have kind of an edge.

Now, we stayed, and those three or four days, close. Amy and I got close and we hung out. It was simple, and I'd do my business, and we'd catch each other for lunch or dinner.

It was just a brief moment where it was in that still unexpressed, undisclosed, unassigned meeting — just their dad and them. We floated in it. And life was given back to us

So '87, it was hard for me, and the drinking became more frequent.

During that following spring and summer, it just—the urge for the disillusion started to creep back in.

Because now Joan, my partner, had developed breast cancer. . .
And now she was in recovery and living on a strict diet and her pain; . . .—it was almost constant.

So that I could remember February and March, and her pain, and she was down but gone away.

I had the boys taken care of.

I'd go for these runs—I'd take the alcohol and I'd go for the run. I'd go off by myself, and I'd go for the run. I'd go for the woods, and I'd go for the run. I'd go for the isolation, and I'd go for the intimacy with myself.

But I didn't know that at the time, but the alcohol worked for me, and was working in a way that I liked it. I wasn't doing it as a way of being ridiculously, stupidly drunk...

But then the need to haunt, and the need to go to haunting places, and the call of people that are caught.

I knew that place, and somehow it was familiar and I liked it, because in my own confusion, I could talk and I could be and I could dominate. I could forget about the pain that was around me.

 So I'd go into bars, and I'd seek people out, and I'd use my aggressive behavior, and I'd dominate them and they'd like it. I'd act with them and they'd like it. I'd be their friend and they'd like it. I'd tell them what they told me, and I'd like it, and I'd cry with them—and they loved that.

I needed the intimacy, and that's one of the things about alcoholics.

Even when we might be fucked up, there's something about our honesty—you can't get rid of it. We go to the bars to drink, because the rest world is insane. We'd get a chance to take the insanity off and sit down and say, fuck that out there, let's get drunk and be happy.

That's kind of — there's another part of that world. Each one of us that are alcoholics know that.

Ninety two percent of the time, the intention is to be happy and free ourselves from some fucking complication we can't get our arms around.

We know that that liquid, that friend would cut us loose.

We don't see any other answers, sometimes, and it's sure and it's fast, and we need it and it works.

When you've got three boys, and a wife with cancer, and 80 accounts; and two daughters you haven't seen in 13 years — I was having a little trouble keeping it together. I had a guru who tore my mind out. I was in that fall, and alcohol allowed me to fall backward into my insanity.

I started to behave like a real alcoholic.

Even though I became a stand-up coach, and the aggressiveness that got cut loose in me, that need to rut was now the need to win, my boys now went out and we kicked ass, we were ruthless, we practiced hard, went to practice, I was into it — didn't make shit for money.

My boys and I went out and we became champions — over and over and over and over again.

They had to earn it, they had to get A's, and they had to keep their room clean, they had to take care of stuff.

They couldn't have girls around until they were 16 !!!

Fuck all the rest of you — young women are predators at that age, they eat these young boys up, grab them by their dick and they don't know what's happening to them.

You women are way more mature, and you don't even know what you're doing — so back up.

I'm telling you. I wouldn't let even incoming calls. I know what's going on, I don't shame you girls, but women take care of that, get in on this game.

These kids can't help themselves — that's a problem here.

We've got to snap it up. This is a moral investigation — yours.

Some lights ought to be going on here.

If you're not clear that I've got a voice of authority from my fucking experience, you know what, I don't give a shit!

What's happening over there?

So in '87, I started.

I didn't have all the right reasons and it worked, kept me calm.

But the hunting, the lack of sex…I started hunting again.

But it wasn't that obvious, yet there was the testosterone and the commitment to go out and get the accounts — it's just coming.

I'm not going to take you through that part, it's not important. I started to cheat in the right places at the wrong time, for all the right reasons.

I needed companionship and intimacy, and my girl was down.

She was really down.

In her sweetness and her softness, there was no tantra; in her wound, in her fear of death, there's not a bit of aggression in me that would want to assault her with some reason to release my tensions.

I knelt at her bed more times than I can tell you, just to hold her.

It was hard for us. You know, just a moment ago…we almost had it

So, I'm a drunk, but I wasn't insensitive, and I wasn't inappropriate.

I was doing the best I could to self-medicate, but the time and the demand just gave me no other quick option—I had to do it in my privacy.

By the time 1990 came along, even though the boys and I were being successful in sports, there came a critical moment where my alcoholism at 2:00 in the morning kicked me right out of Joan's life. Our relationship was terminated right there.

Her father, W. Mark Felt: a retired Associate Director of the FBI, said, "You're gone, get a place now, and don't give me or her any trouble."

I knew what he was talking—it was over, it was a done deal—in 48 hours, I was gone.

So from '90 to '96, I drank and—shitty stories. I'm not going to take you or myself, through that; there's nothing there, except for the incapacity.

But I was already on the bottom in '90. I was there for 10 years. I had software I'd developed. I was always broke and on the edge and borrowing money—and drunk or fighting it.

That's what—I want to skip it up to the event in '97 in the rehab center from '90 to '97, it was just dark, difficult…I don't want to go through the details of—why?

FIFTY-THREE

1997 - REHAB - Suicide or God - Show Me a Sign – NOW

I'm about to share with you an experience that was the — of all the experiences that I have had, I understand this one the most. And yet, because it did happen, sometimes it's difficult to talk about.

In January of 1997, I was in rehab. I had just made a decision that I was going to go ahead and take my life. I was certain; it was clear. I knew where the rope was, I knew where the tree was behind the rehab center. I knew it'd be an awful thing in the morning. But I was made to — okay, because I knew I wouldn't be disturbing anyone anymore, and that I was grateful for everything I'd had.

My mother now was moving into dementia. My boys were getting strong. I was out of answers. My intimate partner was not my intimate partner anymore, and she hadn't been for quite some time, even though I'd been the father to her sons.

In the moment of that clarity, something else occurred — that I was about to extinguish my life. I had given to me the distinction that maybe it wasn't mine to take, because maybe there was a God. I paused — realized that I just had not asked God if He was present. If He was, I hadn't asked to have Him show me a sign — I got it. Before I took my life, I needed to be sure.

I got clear right then. I said out loud, "God, you have to show me a sign right now." Clear piece there — He heard me, right? Just gotta be, just — it's over. God didn't know where I'm at — it's over, right? I knew also that I needed to keep asking. I was going to give it 24 hours and we'll see.

Sometime in the middle of the next morning, I was up on the top of a hill. It'd been my chore to — I had to go up to the top of the hill, and I had to cut down the thistle that was up there.

Part of the chores of the residents is that you had a very strict schedule—rigor, which is important to me: up, meditate, eat, go to work, take a break, talk about AA stuff, and go back to work, eat, have a meeting, go to work, eat, come back, have a meeting, eat. A lot of eating because people's blood sugar was all fucked up. Just the routine normalized everybody—those who would stay.

This was my morning shtick, and I was up in the top of the hill and I was hoeing with a hoe. It was really the top of the crest of a hill in Petaluma, right there where St. Anthony's farm is.

I was not feeling all that well. Things seemed kind of—just as they'd been—kind of semi-numb. I hadn't paid attention to anything in particular, other than kind of the next moment, I noticed one of the cows—one of the female milkers was starting to approach me. I was in animal husbandry, and there are just some animals that like folks and some animals that don't. I could see this animal approaching me, and I could see in her eyes—because I was a livestock judging student for Michigan State—some cows have femininity (check it out, you can see it).

She came over, and I just had this surrender that was completely natural, because I loved dogs. She just bowed her head, and she stuck her head right in the middle of my chest. I dropped this hoe, and just scratched her ears and talked to her, you know—life was good.

All of a sudden, I kind of looked up and the green—God, it was gorgeous day, and the birds are singing—and I'm scratching her, and we're just into it. I'm talking and just the animal talk, and she kind of had enough, but we spent a little bit of time—five minutes anyway.

She went away, and I picked up my hoe. I started to whistle —I hadn't got it yet.

About four minutes later, she came back with seven extra cows, and they all stood around me in a circle, and approached me until they were almost touching me. I became so afraid, because I thought they were going to eat me—I swear to God, I just thought that I'm going to die being eaten by cows.

In kind of the height of the fear, they just turned around and walked away as if nothing was there. I just picked up my hoe and walked down the hill.

It wasn't until that afternoon's meditation that I got the sign. I was leveled, because it was undeniable—life was all around me, and it wasn't my right to take it, I couldn't.

So there you go.

FIFTY-FOUR

The Rapture of My Free Rendering of Sharing

You know—if you got any darkness…? Mine's gone, by the way.

It's a chapter, but in the event of that moment of my life in the '90s, when alcohol took me out of the relationship with Joan and angularized my relationship with my sons—now, they're being put on the high watch, which was good for them.

They got a taste of their loving father, the guy who came in and took them from their cribs, and loved them and held them, and made them champions. No, excuse me, gave them the opportunity to choose to be champions, and they did and they were.

That man changed for them. As they watched that change, it made them cry and angry.

I wrote part of my novel, A Moral Inventory based on that experience of watching my boys shake their head with disgust and turn their back and walk away.

I've still never gotten it back. They moved on.

I got them to 15, I got them to great.

After that, they're on their own anyway!

The organic event of being a father showed up for them, and they got the best of the best of the best, I say. They got a chance to be challenged, and they showed up, and they suited up, and they led.

It wasn't because I told them that they're being taught by anybody. I just asked them questions—do you want it? People don't get it.

We always think you gotta tell somebody something, and then have them repeat it back, and you think that they know something — fuck that. Everybody always knows everything.

Ask them what they want — they'll learn how to speak and use English and math.

Ask them what they want; what do you like?

Most children are too frightened by the intimidation of the challenge to repeat words and symbols; they don't understand the nature of what is already existing, for themselves. They're perfect and whole and complete.

All you gotta do is go, "What do you want?"

People don't get that. They think it's more complicated.

No. What do you want? I love you. What do you need?

See, most parents didn't get what they wanted and they don't have what they need, so they can't ask. Only when you're full and only when you're complete can you turn around and notice others aren't — and you go, "Damn, what do you want?"

And then the process starts. It's just like in recovery. This is just meant to be the interrupt.

The soul of life is alive and well in every human being. What's not there is the invitation to step out, to change the event of where they consider themselves to be by, what do they see.

Most folks can't see what's in front of them, because they've got their eyes in the rearview mirror — back there is some stuff they gotta talk about. Until they talk about it, that rearview mirror's going to be there.

It's not just a motion of get off it. It's a motion of "Turn around, tell me what you see; how does that feel that you're telling me that?"

Be there. Until they go there and be done. When they're done, they'll stand up.

They'll kiss you, they'll turn around, and they'll find someone else.

That's how it works. That's what this is. This is a big turnaround.

I'm turning around with a lot of life experience here, and I'm throwing it at your feet — listen up.

This is your life here, talking back at you. Make some choices. Allow things to be. Find out what's honest for you, and for me, it will help us all recover and discover we're free.

It really is not in the rhyme — it's in the event. It's in the event of unfolding the innocence that's already there, the strength that's already there.

It's not about learning anything new. It's just allowing us to discover what's already true.

FIFTY-FIVE

1997 - Into the Fire My PENNANCE

So, in the late summer of '97, I was hired by a general contractor out of San Francisco. It made a huge difference to me.

I had a friend of mine that I'd known from years past, Kent Argue, and Kent was a really wonderful, sweet son of a very successful pastor in the Santa Rosa area. He and I connected — a very handsome young man. He was maybe 10 years my junior. I've always kind of looked younger, but it's starting to wear on me. Right about that time, most of my hair started to take off south, and the good-looking blond haired kid just turned into a middle-aged man. My chutzpa was leaving, but he and I could still hunt bars together — he was a good lead ticket for me.

But I was still — here we are going into 1997-1998 — damn, man, 50 years old. So, getting to 55 — it's different than just a kid, it's not like a story — it's life, it's real life. It's something it could be — the blending — it's like when I hear my voice — ah, it's the same character — my ass — a hundred different characters, thousands of different moments, just appears to be one person. That kind of orientation to the opening of life had already been created for me, because I never knew what was going to show up.

What did start to show up there was my alcoholism. Even though I'd kind of put it in a can and started to go to AA, it wasn't working. I'd found a couple of ladies that I really dug — they're very attractive in the culture — but they could see I was struggling with the disease.

Everybody knew I was struggling with the disease. My sons were just in shock. They couldn't even stand it anymore. I'd gone to rehab and I was back at it. One boy's getting ready to graduate from high school, and he's beside himself — the disconnect, I don't think we've ever quite recovered from it.

In this drunk-a-log, so much of it is so fucking personal, it's not going to go anywhere except into your ears, but I want it in your ears. If you're going to play with me, if you're going to be with me, you're going to dig with me, you're going to be here — that doesn't have to be for everybody — but everybody who's on that fucking list better be up to speed on this. Put my ass on the line for a good cause.

See, this is an AA meeting for me, I haven't had, isn't it? This whole damn thing is because I haven't had a meeting in five years, right? That's not true. I got my four-year chip last year. That's about it, but I just don't have it.

I'm doing my 12-step work right here, folks. In front of you fine folks, my home group here.

So, my name is Bruce. I'm a recovered alcoholic.

Now, I'm going to stop because I said that on purpose.

Some of the things that I want to highlight, as I start to approach the event of my recovery and the diligence that I was given the opportunity to go through.

I know any of you that like order and form, if you really want to go through the intensity of the true discipline of recovery — just do what you're told — you get a sponsor, you go to 90 meetings in 90 days, and get a big book. Right? Start studying, don't drink. You've got those things.

Now, this leap, these edges around drinking, these conversations about opening it up into, hopefully, the dialogue from that, and others who are listening here can make the connection — that there's other who can't speak, and they can't speak and their behavior speaks. That speaks volumes, as they say.

So, one of the things that happen when I get up to the recovery part — because '97 and '98 was just a dip — it was a dip into the final edges of recovery. I was getting close to the bottom.

FIFTY-SIX

1998 to 2000: ON the Bottom and Digging

But I also know that we're here in 1997, and I'm about to really get into my drinking. I'm giving you the framing of it. I'm giving you — it's starting to hide itself. But now I'm going to start to get partners in it, and I'm starting to get really free. What do I mean by that? I mean, free to choose to find out that I'm on the bottom now, and I'm starting to dig, but I don't get it. It's starting to show up.

I keep going to San Francisco. I go there for my calls, but I may get the last call — could have made it closer to home, couldn't I? I like to be there on Friday, I like that pulse. I like feeling the heat. I like going under cover.

I wasn't going in to hunt or to hunt. I didn't have it in me. I didn't know the bread, man. But I wanted to taste it, I wanted to smell it in a real way. I could do that by sitting down in a bar and buying something cheap, and maybe somebody would like me and buy me a drink.

I started becoming a whore of the night. It was stalking me now, I could feel it, but I couldn't notice it that way — but in retrospect, it was getting me, because it was the only edge. I wanted nothing above my shoulders but the evening, and I wanted nothing else. I didn't want to see anybody; I didn't want to feel anybody. I want to feel the hunt. I wanted to go deep, and I started to go for the hard liquor, and I liked it because it was fast. I only had to get one or two of those things in me to get my engine running. Once my engine got running, I started to do the thing that I loved to do, which was to get gregarious, and then I started to hunt. I'd hunt for the drink, and I'd hunt people; and I'd play them, and I'd play them hard and they never knew. Some did.

Man, I tell you, this one's going to be fun. I'm down in the bowels of San Francisco — I like to turn left, turn right, let's forget about where we are, spin in a circle — where's the next drink? A lot of times, I'd walk into these bars because they were bars that had a lot of action and there was a heat in there. It's like I could be a chameleon and I could sneak in, and I could sometimes steal an abandoned drink. But I was slick and I was fast, and nobody'd see me and no one ever caught me—I was good. I knew this place better than anybody. I'd been on the other side of that bar, I'd been inside that head, I'd been behind that dress of that look—male, that rutting male, and I knew his moves and I could play him by playing into it. I get drunk around them I was having fun getting drunk with kids who were 20 years younger than me.

I could feel the disgust in myself, but I couldn't handle it.

I'd fall out of those places and I'd have to upscale, so I'd move down to the Mission District one time. I got deep down into the bowels of the counter-culture down there. I'd had some close calls with gay people, but I never really wanted to wander there. I even let one guy take me to his apartment—I just wanted to see how far I'd go with him. I was letting it all go, and he gives me the poppers and all the rest of that shit, but he knew I wasn't—I didn't putt in the rough and I wasn't a rocket scientist, so I wasn't going to go down and he knew it. I was just a drunk California boy. I got hit on by a guy like that, but he was kind, he wasn't really a sexual predator—he was a kind, gay man who liked me, but it wasn't happening.

But when I hit San Francisco, I was open to anything. I was open to anything. What showed up was something that I wasn't expecting. There was something inside of me that was true, something inside of me that was accurate, and it was something inside of me that wasn't in the closet, but it was something inside of me that was real. It was something inside of me I didn't know, and I didn't discover it until I fell into this one place.

Man, this place had some really great looking chicks, and I thought, man, these women are outstanding, where are all the dudes? I got myself up to the bar, I think I had myself $50 or $100 with me; I was good for a while. Then I go to the bar, and I'm looking at this gorgeous chick next to me. She's got these long fingernails, and she's doing the thing—it's a little too—I'm starting to get the feeling of…the queen of something. No, no, no, this is not that.

"Honey, you don't have a clue where you're at, do you?"

I said, "What do you mean?"

"Look around, doll."

I went, "What do you mean? Damn, there's not a woman in here." I went, "Oooohhh—oh my God."

Now, it was just unbelievable. I'd never seen she-males before. Man, I had a wonderful night there. I talked and drank and laughed. I felt at home. I wasn't interested in the sex and neither were they, but there was a sisterhood there. There's something about the demand of the mother of the male that says, look, I'm going to kick it up one more level, you bitch punks need to be taken care of, you need to be fathered, need to be mothered first— I'm going to mother you with some serious mother love, and I'm going to show it to you in a dance, but I'm going to actually mother you and I am going to dominate you with love.

I could feel the distinction in the hard core representation of the spike heels and bras, in the hairdo's, and some of them have spent tens of thousands of dollars for the re-do that was gorgeous— everything worked for me with them.

Now, of course, I was drinking; but still—no, no—there was a beauty in the responsibility that those individuals took in the presentations of themselves that caused you to stop at the beauty. One gorgeous Asian man I came up to, and I said, "What do you do during the day, man?" He says, "I'm a stockbroker, nobody has a clue." You could see how he would change his hair, and how it could—and I went, "Ah," and he had breasts. I said, "I gotta tell you, you are incredibly beautiful." I mean, no—physical, because there was something shining through in the fact that they were home as their expression, they were full; there was a radiance that was authentic. I loved being with their authenticity. There's not a— please—it wasn't about any of that.

So anyway, that occasion there at the Black & White or whatever the place was called. You know, that night, it was a—it kind of got me full of the drama, and started giving me an edge of completion with that kind of radical, you know, look — up close and personal, and that edge of people's expression, but more in the drunken lost and found, I just happened to discovery — it wasn't like I was looking for that kind of expression so I could validate it. But I do, because the occasion of the drinking allowed me to be vulnerable enough to live in their world for a few hours. I honor them; their choice of expression is true.

FIFTY-SEVEN

2001 - My Work Begins

So here we are, because I want to launch—I really want to get into the 2001 event—the wonderful swoon of the years at AA had so many wonderful lessons. I so appreciate the opportunity to share them as wonderful lessons. There are a lot of new phrases, things that you get to—that's some of the things I'm going to share is these little snippets that are take-homes.

To shorten up—because there isn't really any value in some of the relationships and wanderings that the bottom held for me that's valuable here—it's painful, it's slow. Even though I had business with friends, the only thing I was able to take what appeared to be a first step, and the first step was to try to break the spell I had with relationships, and the connection I had with people here.

It wasn't working. I had money, but I didn't have the freedom, because there were still my sons and my ex-wife; and my girlfriend and I were starting to get a little autonomy, and I had the ability with my partners to make a final break. I made the jump and I went to Arizona, but I wasn't ready, it wasn't the right time for me there—that wasn't to happen for another year.

I bounced her and I out of there, and put me directly in the line of submission into the AA program in Oklahoma.

When I got there, I was ready.

When I got there, I went to my first contact, because I'd heard about the program and I'd heard about some of the outreaches that they had.

I did made contact with a man that I ended up being close friends with, and still maintain contact with him in our home group back there.

Now you know—I'm on my way, but it's difficult. I have a relationship with a lady who's very sympathetic—to a point. She's not an addict—and yet, at a certain point, even though I was rock solid recovered in my first six months, the constant day-to-day wearing on her of my talking about and sharing about my recovery really got her to the point where she wanted out the back door, even though the person that was showing up was an individual in his first 6, 7, eight months of recovery.

She got to a point, even when I was getting ready to have my first talk at six months, I'm sick of AA—yet, for me, it was one of the most valuable experiences I've ever had.

I'll tell you, the reason being that you think it'd be a natural, normal thing to continue to say in the future, having had your friend who traveled with you for three years watching you bounce off the bottom—when you're getting ready to have your first AA meeting and you invited her, and she goes, I'm sick of AA.

My feelings were hurt. I went in the bathroom, taking a shower, getting ready to go the meeting, and I was proud, I was happy, I couldn't wait. I heard some things from the individuals preparing for that meeting, and I thought, that's great, tell people something funny and start in the middle of it and just go.

And yet, I was there in the shower, and I was resentful, pissed. I'd worked hard, and I'd gone through my fourth step, and it was hard. I'd busted my ass to get to my fourth step, and I started right—I was in my fourth step with inside of 72 hours of hitting the pavement. My sponsor grabbed me by the ass, gave me a yellow pad, and had me into the fourth step—I promise you—within 90 seconds of asking me the first question: Was I ready?

I was on. He had me sponsoring people in two days. That's just how that was, and that's how lethal it was back there. They call them AA Nazi, in the right way. They didn't take prisoners. They took your heart; they got you through it.

So I'm in the shower, and I'm having this intense resentment. I realized how much work I'd gone through to get rid of all my resentments—semi-resentment—I was resentful, but I noticed there was a before and an after. I was in that point, I was getting ready to notice that I was going to put this in a familiar place where I stored things — kind of like my resentment file draw, and I'd pull it out and go, "Oh, yeah, yeah, K — K — Katharine — oh yeah, Katharine, on November 19, 2001, you didn't..." — and I was that serious. I was getting ready to kind of log it, so I could go back and reference it, so I could use it. Because as a liar, you've got to get ammunition to back up the transference of the irresponsibility you have to tell the truth, but whatever the hell you're dealing with in the moment that you're trying to tell a story that someone did it to you before — wrong move if you want to get into recovery.

The first thing you've got to do is you've got to notice if you've gotten clean — I'm talking psychologically — shit, the alcohol's easy. Stay sober for six months and go to a meeting for six months, every day for six months, for six months. Yeah, right. You want to really recover?

That's what you do, or you die. I got that.

324 meeting in 365 days — forget about it, I don't give a shit, but I did it — 124 in 90, I did it.

Now, she's not going to go, and I'm going to — and I went, no, no, no — and I got it. I had a choice: I could choose to just drop it — or — all the rest, typical thing, the thing that we do — pack it away, give it a title, line it up in the list, in the zipper that hasn't been unzipped of all things you've got connected that are your resentments and angers, and you haven't unzipped it because you've still got this armor on you — me, I had at the time.

That was the cool part, and that's the essence, and that's the great part about recovery — it's just so much deeper than most people are willing — you can't get it until you get it. That's why all the people that are in recovery that are listening me that are going, "Yeah, you know, because I am telling it with a swagger, and it is fun, it is real, and it is right on."

I'll tell you, the people in recovery have an appreciation for me. I haven't even had one person hear anything, but I know — you want the passion for getting laid? Passion in recovery is way — man, it takes you over with the joy and the passion of caring, the passion of serving, the passion of listening and watching and participating — the great allowing of passion, the forgiveness of passion. Passion isn't just this hot searing, you know, dance of hot heels and romance. It's not a flamenco event. Passion isn't always like that. It's not something that's all red and orange and pointed. It's soft and blue and gentle, and it touches your brow in the form of your mom or your girlfriend.

It's the living passion.

This is the conscious event of talking about it, ruthlessly. You know — why not — why not wander with me in this event of the inspection of it all? There aren't any more wild stories. But there is the finishing — the getting to the occasion of the gentle commitment to say in the recovery, because everything it's told is true. The promises are all true. Before you're halfway through, there is a — it's a whole brand new game. You can't get there from here, or you can't get here from there — because if you're not here, if you're not present, you're there, and that hurts because there is a here, and there's a distinction for you who heard me. All of us who've been there know it. It's not an abstraction. It's a hurtful distance. You can come here, and you can be here, and you can be alive here and forget there. But there are duties to pay, responsibilities and amends to make.

In AA, I had an opportunity to hear men talk — lots of men talk, and lots of men walk the walk. We went to meetings all the time; we went to meetings every day — twice a day, 12:00, 6:00 — 124 in 90, do the math. It's not that hard. When you're in the swoon, and your back is against the wall, and you have someone of strength that you reach out for and say, "Will you help me?" and the individual looking back at you, steel-eyed, rocket science presence saying, "Hello. Are you powerless over alcohol; has your life become unmanageable?" "Uh-huh." "You take the first step." You can't get any — you can't even talk about the second step even in this consideration here, because that's not what it's about.

But I was able to — with Jimmy Gent — I was able to take the first, second, and third step right there in his presence. He asked me if I was "willing to life and will over to the care of God as I understood

Him?" Yeah, I was ready. I knew there was a power greater, but I couldn't feel it.

To me, it was God in that group of drunks.

These guys, man—talk about a brotherhood. They're still there for me—every one of them. I feel them in my heart. I know their stories. That brotherhood of the recovered soul that still stands in the wound with his own armor still half off, reaching back to those that have none that are down—you know, they're down, they're hard. Those are the guys you would go see every Sunday—Jimmy and I and Tom Pace and a lot of good men.

Tom Pace sponsored 20 guys at a time—he's an amazing human being, still active. I'd never give up their anonymity and it'd never come out on tape, but you're going to hear those names from me. If you go to Oklahoma right now, you want to get sober—go see Jimmy Gent or Tom Pace—done deal. You don't have to have anything—walk, run—they've got your back. They'll find you a job and they'll put you to work, but you've got to turn it over—do not plan to go anywhere for at least one year, if not two. That's the pay-it-forward. But you walk out with your life, you want out with your mind in the proper place as something you use that doesn't use you because you've mis-used it.

There are dues to pay when you don't pay attention to the law, and you know the law—you can't say and do stuff that's irresponsible, it comes back, it doesn't work.

That's what's the communication when things don't work—that's the message—it doesn't work, don't do that anymore.

People go, "I can't help it." Good, get help.

The thing most of all is, you've got to deal with this, you've got to deal with this—the arrogance that people have in the face of all evidence that they're just not going to choose to be sober. If they're too close to you, you gotta walk back. If they're not willing to hear it, walk back—but you can't yell at them, you can't make them wrong because they're sick. They're sick, they're sick.

That, if anything else, if you're not familiar with AA, if you're not familiar with any kind of recovery, if you're not familiar with addiction — it's not like I'm saying they're sick, like, a color or a label — they're ill. They've lost the capacity to discriminate between what makes sense, and the face of the fact that they have a habit that doesn't work and they're just denying it. Denial is the first part of the illness.

Once the denial snaps off, recovery initiates, if the person can take a step. Some people can hang with the disease and continue to feed it, and that's the horror, because then everybody's sucked into that — then it's gotta go pro. You've got to be serious. Lethal — it's going to happen to you, or you do it. You must be proactive. That was the message, because we'd go to first step, and we'd go to these guys that are out there in the DOC, and that's the hard line, these guys got prisoner this. And we went there every Sunday, and Jimmy was great, he is great. I don't know how active he is about it, but I'm telling you, these guys are just — been going here six years — six years, every Sunday, for somebody else after they go to church with their family in the morning. They miss — it takes them 45 minutes to get there. Do the math — hour and a half. They go pick up sponsees and take them. Some have to leave at 4:30 to be there at 6:30. Okay, do the math. Hours and hours and hours of dedication, these men — that's recovery.

It isn't one hour a week in a meeting with a sponsor, and not drinking. Excuse me. I take license — not if you've been on your knees, bottom-feeding drunk. I hate to push like this, but this is it. I'll edit and take and chop out of it; but when you're at that level and you're on the bottom and you don't know, somebody has to take your food away from you. Sometimes it is lockdown, detox — but Lord, you know.

Most of you — no one close to this is planning to be that desperate. Denial is not just for the person who's sick. It's not a river in Egypt.

We've got this event of allowing the person to approach you in the first step. That's what this journey is now, and it may be a first step for you, too.

These stories — these times now that I'm expressing — are the lay down of the event of the revelation of my own insight into the pattern of becoming. What does that mean? Becoming more conscious. What does that mean? That means that I notice my life as I went along. What does that mean? Listen.

So that's the event. This is when I call you and I say to you, the knee of listening, like my guru said to me, it really is. It's something we do. We need to be at the knee of it, which means that we're paying attention with a sense of respect; that whatever's speaking, we give authority to it with our ears. We place the knee there, now we're listening. But it's an action, it's a behavior, it's an opening, it's an inquiry. So these stories are really like — that's why they're screwed through with the demand to stay with the free-fall. If you stay with the free-fall, you don't get caught in what did that mean — you just stay with the free-fall. And, if you re-listen, you're going to see that there were stories and impacts.

But I do want to have this sense of speaking without pause with you, because this how it's happening. I may come out — the thing I have to send these things, you see, in little 5-minute snippets, but I haven't stopped talking for whatever, and I don't want to continue…Every time I stop this this night, January 14-15, it pauses. I'm just back at it now. This can be a 7-8 hour ordeal. I'm going until done. So, get it, get it. There's the message, and I'm holding the space of the context of the completion of this drunk-a-log.

But forgiveness that I have for the individual that holds that place in my memory, throws me into a rapture, and I get a little lost. I can't go back and listen to it anymore, and I can't go back and edit these titles anymore, and I can't put chapters on, and I'm going to tend to go forward in the chronological order — but I can't — and I'm going to break them up to email them, but they're just going to come in bunches, and they're going to come contiguous to time.

So, the only thing it is — and I don't want to have anything held back for any of you who are participating in the dynamic of the immediate listening of this — if anyone is. I don't want to be more than a few hours away from the download, because it's that raw to me. I need to respect my vulnerability, and the commitment I have to move through it. I just hold the space of the immediate listening of those who do listen, but I can't go back and listen to them anymore — I just can't.

We're on our own here. Thank you for the patience of putting up with whatever this good idea I have has. If anybody gets any value — one guy doesn't drink for the rest of his life because he heard something along the way — that'd be enough. I don't need any money — I don't. You can tell I have the grace of perspective, and I have the courage to tell people of incredible respect in their industries. I couldn't expose myself to anything less than what I consider to be the highest listeners available, and I didn't know that, but I know that.

So this is the confession of a soul — and it's raw sometimes — but it's just what's there. The lack of the sense of it, but there's a continuity when the rapture starts. It's a song that the soul has to sing, and I feel it. It's like I've sung it before, is the message that I sit on the edge of. But it's like, I'm willing to be the sacrifice in the 21st century, you know. Someone else did it — it's not in the fucking books, and there isn't an experience that I've had that every one of us have had. It's just — I'm in the reflection and that's it, and there's the value. It's about looking at the thread of the life form, and the thread of the joy, and not the condemnation for some puritanical right to belong to society.

And yes, we're on the hunt to control alcohol.

So, thank you for listening. Like I said, I won't listen to this. But from here on out, as I merge into that character that stands above that young man and I allow that theater of his gentleness to inform the oration of the story. But when I go back, I'm gone, and I can't go back and then go back to edit. I've said it enough.

Thank you for being here for me.

FIFTY-EIGHT

The Initial Signs of Sobriety – OTHERS WANT YOU AROUND

One of the features of knowing that you're sober is being able to have others recognize a quality about your seriousness and restedness that they invite you to be in their life, and the people know you've been drinking. Those who are not close to AA have huge respect for people that are six months to a year sober; that we, in the program, know that that's just the beginning of a long journey, and that a year is nothing. It doesn't mean to diminish — my God, a year is the commitment — you've got to do a year, it doesn't happen, not if you've been drinking and out of control and you fucked things up.

Gabriel — really, when I got to nine months — not like nine months was something — I got a year in, and Gabriel Cousens called me. All of a sudden, there I was — I was transformed.

Okay, here you go: Went on a men's retreat, April 12, 2002. I had very little money, and Catherine and I were kind of okay, but I didn't have a focus or a career. I gave my — I said, "God, you know, give me a sign, what do you want me to do?" Well, would you know when I get home from the retreat, I'm walking into Penny's where Catherine's working, and who calls me on my cell phone? Gabriel Cousens. What does he want to do? He wants to hire me as his manager.

There in Oklahoma, I was thoroughly bathed in the rituals of AA, solidly for a year, giving me enough clarity and sobriety — such that I was ready to have a job in Arizona.

With the goodwill of my sponsor and my one-year chip, I was out there, and I was off to Arizona, and off to a live with Dr. Gabriel Cousens.

Well, wave that magic wand and get to the bottom of the story and get on with what it feels like to be in recovery.

That's what it is—you get people of quality that ask you to be with them in recovery. They know that you've done something; they appreciate it; they want you to give them your life and support.

The life with Gabriel Cousens was very ordered. It was beautiful. It was exactly what I wanted. It was a true spiritual retreat for me. I'd made that break from the dull routines of the everyday world, and the chase after the money. I felt like I'd made my mark in regards to software, and I'd done something. I had a relationship with a good woman that I basically had to cut her loose because she was dysfunctional, and I could see that, and I had to be responsible for it.

These are some of the things that are hard to say, but again, I'm trying to go through these things, and I don't want to be caught in the editing of it—I want to be caught in the flow of the release.

I want to stay on target until I get this damn thing out of me.

So here we go. Gabriel was good, and he was awesome. He was a great teacher—I learned a lot from him, learned the term inauthentic, inauthentic person. That's true, you know, we have this sometimes a made-up personality and belief and ideas about who we think we are, and we act it all out and we present it as a personality with a story and time, and yet, trying to keep that all together, that's who you present. You hear about that, but it's so true—I'm a football player or this—it's not what we're talking about in recovery. The football player does not score another touchdown, nor does the divorcee get married again.

What happens is, a form of sanity gets grounded—it gets grounded because the person gets out of the silliness of paying attention to any abstracting stories that tells them anything about more survival is in getting it in order from that perspective—it'll never happen that way. That's part of the thing—because no one's in on the recovery, no one knows what the sanity is. Most people are kind of fairly clear about the insanity, but it's the sanity part, and you don't see the distinction ever until, all of a sudden, you've gotten so far away from the bottom that there's a miracle that occurs—that's what's starting to occur for me. I hadn't completed it, but you start to see the sharp distinction.

Now, with Gabriel, I was very occupied. As an alcoholic, for me, I'm very A-type, I'm very proactive. As I started to get his business together, which really occupied me for about 8-9 months, and I did well and saved him hundreds of thousands of dollars, hired him great staff, reorganized, got him out of huge debt, got rid of some bad LLCs. I was feeding on the multi-tasking.

What was happening was that there was a hunger starting to occur because I wasn't being satisfied, really. It wasn't enough. It wasn't enough that I was doing Gabriel well, I still didn't have a sense of myself, and I was doing all the things that he was recommending. I was doing all the disciplines, but the raw was a little too intense, in that he was so critical on raw—shit, I was doing coffee, and caffeine is so clean that one cup of coffee a day just kept me wracked.

There was no alcohol at all. I was on just hyper-vitamins and raw food. So the energy was good and the company was outrageous.

But, when Gabriel went away a few times, there was this passion in me because everything was in order. I'd seen that as the key to the background of my going out, because then there wasn't enough to keep me occupied. I went back for the dissolution. I went back for the dissolution that came with the guarantee that alcohol would give it to me.

I knew that, but I didn't know that, and I didn't know again I was trying to get to that dissolution again.

It wasn't enough that I was clean and sober; it wasn't enough that I had the dream of the lifetime job, that this guy turned his business over to me. I promise you, something wasn't right.

It wasn't right, and eventually a year plus later, I got found out, and it wasn't pretty.

So I immediately went back to Oklahoma to reestablish my AA practice ...before I moved back to Northern California in 2005.

FIFTY-NINE

2001 - Recovery Begins: November 11, 2006, The Miracle Happened for Me

So in that moment, the miracle happened for me. On November 11, 2006, the miracle happened for me.

I had the occasion to throw out the last bottle of wine — it was a good bottle — started to get into the Pinot. See, I was still on that edge, I was still bouncing it. But I'd gone to meetings, see. I'd been working it and back in it, and I knew I was close to something.

Also, what had happened is that I had begun counseling and Science of Mind. I'd been into both for about a year, and I started using the Empowerment Groups to learn to pray - direct your own life by keeping your word . . .

It's really invoking life: by using your word.

That relationship to my life up to that moment on November 11 was starting to be dominated like I wanted to be dominated by a living relationship. Because of my sense of my organizing principles, I feel I want to be part of order — not an order in the thought, but an order in people and an alignment, I want to listen to messages by others in group. I like the response and the camaraderie of the discussion of the impact of things that are said — we've got an awesome minister, just the best in Edward Viljoen.

During that time, I felt him and I needed him, and I went through an organic event — again, the practice of prayer. It's the use of the word, just our word, and I started letting go of stuff — the alcoholism was falling back, the use was way, way back until this moment.

And then, on the day of my mother's AA birthday, and this event of throwing out the bottle of wine — because I smelled the choice, it was different. That's the distinction that anybody, a child has—when you smell alcohol, if you're a child—I mean, if you're a drinking alcoholic, or even if you drink—take a bottle of rubbing alcohol and smell it—take a big-ass whiff. Okay. You won't be able to handle it, will you? No, you won't. That event, to a clean, recovered alcoholic is the same event—you can't get close to it, it hurts—it hurts more than just in the nostrils.

The miracle event for me is so psychophysical, that it represents a door into an experience. It's just like, you want another 20 years?—even though it doesn't say that. The sting—you can't even get close to your nose.

If you're recovering, you're not going to do it.

But the ED is you can't do it. I can't—I cannot—I cannot consider bringing alcohol to me, in my hand, to me, with the intention of consumption, because it won't do for me what I want—I want more. It will—no, it will take it away—it'll give me less. It won't give me more.

I know the distinction, and I have so much more because I've let go of all the baggage.

Now, can you imagine your life if you haven't dropped the baggage—to be baggage-less and totally forgiven absolutely and clean and sober, and no money complaints—none/zero—for the rest of your life?

That's me.

That's ED—we're not talking about that one.

I'm talking recovered…

Now, here's that story—you get little stories—here's one to take with you on this: So what's the difference? I tried to describe it to you in the form of the smells and the experience, and the distinction that I have repulsion—literally.

That's the miracle. I can't cause that.

If I were a drinking alcoholic, would I have a repulsion? No. I mean, if it were bad wine, sure.

If I'm a practicing alcoholic, which means I'm using alcohol frequently or not, if that was the only thing left, I'm going for it—the alcoholic.

This is not that.

I keep dwelling around it, because I keep wanting people to get to, "What do you mean, what do you mean, what do you mean?"

I've tried to tell you—it's a shift in the willingness to have things go in me, that I don't like the smell of, or the taste of.

I'm pretty good about—I like bitter things—shit, I drink cod liver oil.

I don't have a problem with difficult-tasting good stuff.

And, here's the story:

What's the difference between a recovering and recovered alcoholic?

What's the difference between a recovering and a recovered gunshot wound victim?

They're recovering, right? They had the wound.

Is there going to be a point in which that individual says, "I'm recovered?" Well, probably, right? The tissue will be repaired, bone will be repaired—it wasn't that bad that it didn't tear the bone out.

So you're going to be recovered.

So, there's a point at which, if you've done the ninth step—and I've done it twice—ninth—eighth, ninth, tenth—especially the ninth step—gotta do those amends, man. You gotta know what it means to recognize your emotions and discriminate them in a fourth step, and you can't do it!

If you haven't done them, you don't know. If I haven't bungee-cord jumped, I don't know. If you haven't gone through the 12 steps, that's one thing; if you are in an addiction situation and you haven't gone through the fourth step, you ain't going to get there from here — ain't going to get here from there — can't, because the block is in the way it's wired in, and you got the wiring.

You've got to unwire it, and that's — you've got to turn it over in order to have that happen.

Most people don't, and they won't — they won't take the confront. They just keep the alcohol in the place, and they tell you to get the fuck away from me. That's what the behavior will show you — "Stay away from me!"

And; a recovered (**ED**) alcoholic is you don't drink anymore.

Now, gunshot victim, all right — recovered . . **ED**

Alcoholic gone through an eighth, ninth, tenth step — recovered **ED**

Now, is that person bulletproof? No!

Is the alcoholic drink proof? No!

Do both have choice to not put themselves in the line of fire?

What's the answer to that?

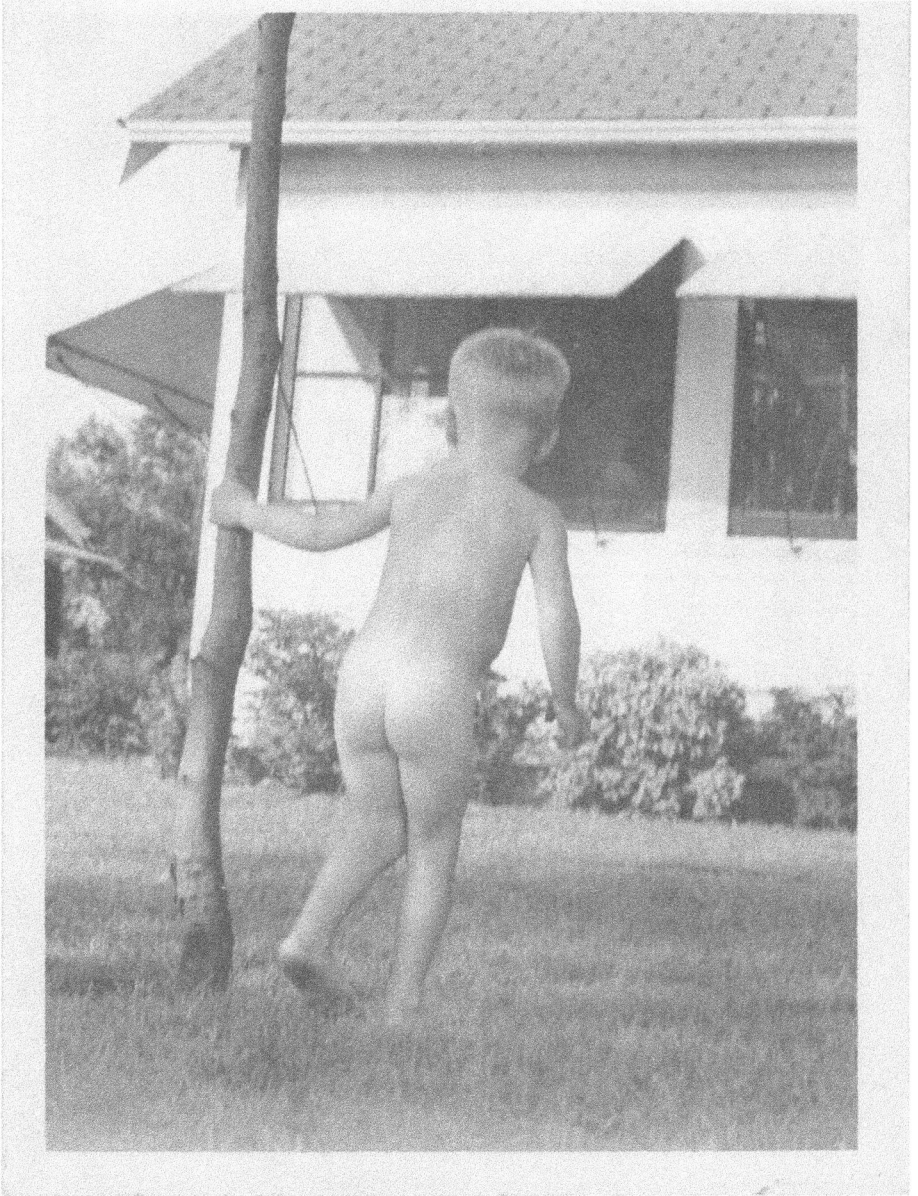

My mother loved this photo of me in Canada in the summer of 1948; always kept it on her dresser...she was 20 months sober...almost all of the photos here included were from my mother's many, many photos and albums ...She would be so happy others are seeing them ...that I am well, healthy, happy and sober !

Grosse Pointe Spartans Football * Ken Davis – Einstein's Relativity
Poor grades so: U of Michigan TESTS: 135 IQ College Math Level
My sister Ruthie, Nora Adams; my mammy, our maid w/ me @ 12

Best wishes for a
Merry Christmas

Boy my mom loved me . . . never did she ever: criticize me - EVER
My mom related LOVING TO ACTION
SHE ENCOURAGED OTHERS TO LOVE . . . NOW

"I need 10 new hugs today honey; on her way to an AA meeting !

My son Robby Jones made this for me, knows me very well
He and his brothers got a dad; we had A Wonderful Life
Grounded in Love & Graced by God - -ALWAYS PLAY & FUN

Robby: ALL STAR Catcher: 1992 Santa Rosa District 35
Batted over 650: 18 triples, 12 doubles and 8 Home Runs

My Other Source these days: just like my mother
My living EXAMPLE of strength, hope & courage IN ACTION
My wife Carol a sponsor & recovered food addict

"If God had meant man to fly; he would have given him wings
. . . OR . . .
the truth doesn't mean anything; . . . it just is !"

. . . Werner Erhard: Up To Your Ass in Aphorisms - circa 1978